PRAISE FOR *THE DIFFERENCE BETWEEN SEEDS & STONES*

"Exquisitely written, this book is a testament to the power and expansiveness of the human spirit. Ostensibly, this is a memoir of Rondi Lightmark's personal journey through the pain and grief of her husband's death to engage with the reality of the post-mortem world. Beyond her story, though, she has crafted a compelling exploration of the spiritual depths within each of us which can open to the miracle and wonder of Life all around us, Life that knows no end and has no limits on its blessings. This book is a jewel of inspiration."

—David Spangler, author of *Apprenticed to Spirit*
  and *Blessing: The Art and Practice*

"Rondi Lightmark's intimate account of her husband's illness and death offers a new way to experience loss and grief. Her stories show that the death of a loved one is not the end of consciousness and connection, but can bring us closer to the world of spirit, turning our grief into an opportunity to heal our souls."

—Carol Bowman, author of *Children's Past Lives*
  and *Return from Heaven*

"A memoir is much more than an author's life story when we can learn from it, grow from it, and see ourselves in it. In *The Difference Between Seeds and Stones*, Rondi Lightmark succeeds in all three ways. Her views of spirituality are not esoteric, or superficial and fluffy, or mainstream, or even radical. Instead, there is something for everyone on this amazing journey called life. We will all die; we will all grieve loved ones who pass before us. How to authentically grieve in the most evolved manner possible is what we are taught, in a humble and real way."

—Judith Miller, Ph.D., author of *Healing the Western Soul*

"In this remarkable book, Rondi Lightmark charts a journey that she embarked on when her husband fell ill and passed on, a journey that began with grief but continued as an adventure of spiritual growth and her development as a talented writer. It is illustrated with dreams, poems, song lyrics, keepsakes, and synchronicities. It chronicles Rondi's inner feelings and external adventures, all of which she shares with her readers. For Rondi, stones represent past histories, seeds represent future possibilities, and how adroitly she has navigated between both of them."

—Stanley Krippner, coauthor of *Personal Mythology* and
    Extraordinary Dreams and How to Work with Them

"One of the author's pastimes, as revealed in *The Difference Between Seeds and Stones,* is gardening, and she has no doubt drawn upon her horticultural skills in cultivating this beautiful garden of the heart from the soil of love. The book is much more than a magnificent tribute to an extraordinary relationship, though that in itself would make it worth the read. We are taken on a profound journey of grief, recovery, and transcendence. While it is the author's story, it is rich with portals into the deeper human adventure and its spiritual foundations. You will be riveted and enriched by reading it."
—David Feinstein, coauthor of *Personal Mythology* and *The Energies of Love*

THE DIFFERENCE BETWEEN
SEEDS & STONES

RONDI LIGHTMARK

LightmarkArts

VASHON ISLAND, WASHINGTON

LightmarkArts / Rondi Lightmark
www.rondilightmark.com
RondiLTMK@gmail.com

Cover design by Kristine Dahms/Twistdesign.biz
Copy editing and book production by Stephanie Gunning

Special discounts are available to librarians and on quantity purchases by corporations, associations, and others. For details, contact the publisher.

Library of Congress Control Number: 2023902029

The Difference Between Seeds and Stones / Rondi Lightmark —1st edition

ISBN 979-8-9877209-0-5 (paperback)
ISBN 979-8-9877209-1-2 (kindle ebook)

CONTENTS

The First Question: BODY
Will Grief Kill Me?

The Second Question: SOUL
Who Am I Without My Beloved?

The Third Question: SPIRIT
What Is My Source of Strength?

Seeds & Stones
November 12, 2022

GATHERING

My life, like a span of geese, gathers
each night at your door

You condense me to presence and
open the heart of rest, meaning
a deep arc of simple heat.

You watch the way
to sleep.

Later, in the blank throb
of peace, there is
a delicate burn that rustles
leaves of soul.

We slip our skins to
hunt the leaning birches, to
shout the falling distance, to wear
the spill
of flight

Only a moon's draught of space, a feather-beat
of breath
is where our edges know
this death.

PRELUDE

....

HERE IS JIM

A brown mustache serves as a prop for his devilish, flirty grin, inviting delight, hinting misbehavior. Dark brown eyes, soft brown hair, a faraway gaze in quieter moments, warm voice, slight build. Our legs are the same length, but my torso kept growing two more inches, while his is more compact. He makes up for the difference with his big hug. His arms are long and his hands are big, with pronounced knuckles—no doubt the result of swinging a hammer. He is trained as an architect, but loves to build, feels that if he's going to frame a building on paper, he needs to get his hands on it as well.

On his father's side, he's related to Johnny Appleseed, that barefoot pioneer nurseryman who sowed scripture and seed for hard cider crops throughout the Midwest in the 1700s. James Robert Chapman is the man I marry. The vagabond waste-not-want-not is woven into his soul somewhere, most evident in his old worn, brown leather shoes, his treasured, almost transparent tee-shirts and a closet so packed with textile memorabilia that our first fight is about how I have no room for my clothes.

We are both thirty-three when we meet at Emerson College in southern England. It's a place for studying the work of the Austrian philosopher, scientist, and spiritual teacher Rudolf Steiner (1861–1925), whose worldview, called *anthroposophy* ("wisdom of man") inspired numerous social, cultural, and artistic endeavors. These include the international Waldorf School movement, anthroposophical medicine, and biodynamic agriculture.

Despite a successful career, Jim is at Emerson searching for a different path, one that will include children and teaching. He is in his second year of a training course. I've come to England on sabbatical, utterly spent from teaching and working as an administrator at a Waldorf high school in New Hampshire while in a collapsing marriage, and with a bad case of imposter syndrome that was taking me apart at the seams. I've been at the school since I was twenty-three, but have had no life experience or formal education for the roles I've been invited to play. I originally came by dint of having married my husband, a man seven years my senior. His uncontrollable temper eventually got him fired, while I stayed on.

I'm here at Emerson under rather false pretenses. While I do want to study Steiner's philosophy more deeply, there is that other issue, that imposter piece. I feel like I've never really grown up. My real agenda, therefore, is to extricate myself from my explosive marriage while journeying far from the familiar, both inwardly and outwardly, until I can discover where the real Rondi is hiding herself.

Jim comes with a wealth of countercultural experiences, high ideals, and treasured friends and family. His life has been defined in good part by his feisty, humorous, and challenging mother, Stella, who was given the name Mammy by his only sibling, Barbara. Mammy's ancestors came with Daniel Boone through the famous Cumberland Gap in the Appalachians and they'd settled to work as sharecroppers in Kentucky. They were a hardworking, hard-playing Scotch-Irish tribe, "poor as dirt."

Mammy was born in the middle of a line of twelve sisters and brothers, but with an intelligence and innate fire that gave her precedence among her siblings. She cried for a week when she had to quit school and go to work during the Great Depression and she never got over her hunger for learning, completing her GED when she was nearly seventy.

Smart, self-sacrificing, both tough and tender, Stella raised Jim to wrestle rather than to hug. He had to figure the hugging out himself after he made the mistake of enthusiastically tackling some bigger guy's girlfriend in high school. Mammy adored him and he cherished her, while bearing a lasting psycho-emotional debt due to her many insistent self-sacrifices on his behalf.

We meet in an entryway at the college, in front of a lively watercolor Jim has painted of waves breaking on the island of Iona, Scotland, which I am admiring. The spark that ignites the two of us full-time is the discovery that we both like to be very, very silly. Our styles mesh perfectly. Since childhood, we've both been mimics, hams, quipsters—spontaneous stagers of our own nonsensical dramas.

But Jim also has a core story that he shares with me early on. When he was very young, he felt the constant presence of angels—until a time in the bathtub when he was maybe five or six, and they all washed down the drain when the plug was pulled. He screamed and screamed then, and would not be consoled. The shock and sense of loss seems to have marked him lifelong with the sense that he was a stranger in a strange land. There was an indigo streak of sorrow threaded through his soul, a hint of unspent treasure buried deep because he felt there was no room for it to emerge in the family his soul had chosen.

His complexity of light and dark powerfully draws me in, and to be in his presence is a deep, almost scary, thrill.

At the end of my sabbatical, I return to my job at the Waldorf high school and Jim follows soon after to work as an intern in the eighth-grade middle school class. Back home, with Jim on my turf, we continue to feel the deep pull between us. However, my fierce desire to break away from the life I have known since

I was barely out of high school takes me out of state a year later, after my divorce, leaving Jim behind.

I am brave not to leave my mark on him. Single women quickly fill in the gap my absence creates. With his wit, sparkle, and innate kindness, he is a major chick magnet. I have taken a job ninety minutes away at a progressive boarding high school in Vermont, and am raising my two teenage children alone.

My ex-husband, their father, has departed for adventures out West, after declaring that if I don't do a good job with "his kids," he'll come back and kill me.

Three years go by and my teenagers graduate from their new high school, leaving me sobbing, the first time over songs about children growing up (my daughter), and the second time, over the discovery of a big pile of beer cans in a bush under my son's window (misplaced nostalgia).

All the while, Jim and I keep reconnecting, finally realize it's forever, and marry the year after my nest has emptied, even as his architectural work increases in the community I've left. There has been a devastating fire in the Waldorf elementary school sited about five miles away in a nearby town. Putting his dreams of leading a class on hold, Jim returns to architecture to help build a new elementary school on a property adjacent to the high school where I had formerly been working. He spends much of our first year together finishing the school, surrounded by grateful, dedicated parents and faculty.

Jim's approach to architecture is inspired by Steiner's work of creating spaces that have organic, evolving energy. He designs the school to inspire and foster the potential of the children and teachers therein. When it is completed, the result is a triumph of a building and the pinnacle of his architectural career.

With the school in New Hampshire finished, we settle into making a home in southern Vermont, turning an ugly manufactured log cabin on the Green River into an enchanting, shingled cottage surrounded by flowers that grow rampant in the moist air of our valley. Having never gone to college, I take time off from working a side job as a waitress to enroll. A few years later, I will earn a self-designed bachelor's degree in the art and science of human language under the auspices of a program at the University of Massachusetts at Amherst.

The years turn around a few times as we work on our home and our relationship deepens. And then, we are awakened one night to hear that Jim's school, the glorious auditorium just completed, is ablaze. A final coat of finish had been put on the stage flooring and the oily rags piled in a heap outside, far from the building, in a field. But in the middle of the night, a heavy wind came up, blew those rags into a terrible fiery mass, and pushed it onto one of the school porches.

By morning, the new auditorium is gone, both wings of the school are damaged, and the school has to close. Insurance is supposed to cover a rebuild, but this time, despite continued love and support from parents and faculty, Jim is threatened with lawsuits and the loss of his reputation and career by the insurance company, which is hoping to find fraud so they won't ever have to pay up.

The tragedy and rancor nearly break Jim's heart. In a way, it's more angels down the drain. It is fortunate that I then find myself enticed back into Waldorf education.

Jim has not given up his dream to become a teacher. And I don't want to teach anymore, but there is a new Waldorf kindergarten in Vermont looking for one and I love Jim and want to support him. I say yes, but only if Jim joins me as a co-teacher, since he lacks the experience to take on a class by himself.

There we are, frolicking with twenty creative, energetic five- and six-year-olds. Waldorf kindergarten is an immersion in wonder and imaginative play with lots of storytelling and celebrations of Nature in every season. Jim and I channel our innate playfulness into telling stories, leading songs, rituals, plays, games, and festivals. We bake bread, make soup, do simple sewing and finger knitting, paint watercolors, and model with colorful, fragrant beeswax. Each year is more fun, more creative, than the last.

We carry on like this for three years. Until the Unthinkable happens.

THE FIRST QUESTION

BODY

WILL GRIEF KILL ME?

MOON IN DARK WATER

9.19.93

It's midnight and freezing. The heavy rumpling of the river is only a few feet away from me in the blackness, while at the far end of the meadow, the light of one lamp in our living room window shines softly out into the night. Inside, Jim is lying on our foldout couch and his friend Ed is keeping watch.

While Jim is dying.

I'm out here, breathless and afraid, pressing my body and face hard against a tree, playing a tragic game of pretend. The tree is about as big around as Jim, and within my gesture there is the whimpering acknowledgment that Jim will never push against me, put his arms around me, ever again.

Our house is perched on a little rise on the edge of the Green River, which surges by at its base, heading east out of the mountains for a few miles and then south beyond Vermont. A strand of the river is channeled into the center of a small meadow, forming a serene pool about fifty feet long behind me. Jim made the pond when we bought the house because he said our land needed to include a place of stillness near running water or else—as the Chinese counsel—our good fortune would wash away downriver.

It's too soon for bitterness.

This is the first time that I've been away from Jim's side since the first of August, that day I stood in the road and watched the ambulance pull away from me. And then, the hours I sat in the waiting room at the hospital, while Jim had tests that showed that the seizure had occurred because the cancer from the melanoma had finally crept into his brain. And then, the doctor saying to go home and call hospice and the two of us alone in the elevator after, me clinging to Jim and wailing: *Oh no oh no oh no.*

Two months since then, refusing to give up, trying to hold him when he hurts, even trying to get him in my lap like a child, to just hang on, to push all of my health and heart into him.

All year, I've wanted to run up to strangers and demand they admit that they too have a life in this parallel universe of horror. I've fantasized putting up a sign in our local Vermont town: HONK IF YOU KNOW SOMEONE WHO IS DYING OF CANCER! I imagine a sounding day and night until we'd have to put all else aside and make it stop.

But now, there's only Jim and everything it means to lose him, to know that someday soon, I will know the sullen weight of death in my arms.

The breath of the river is sliding across our land, and it smells of frost. There's a cloud across the moon in a night with a few intermittent stars. I move to wander aimlessly across the grass, scuffing the clumps of dead lupine that flood the meadow with blue in the spring. I'm searching for a way to go back inside, to face the days ahead. There's the memory of the doctor in our living room tonight, looking down on Jim and saying flatly, "It'll be a while yet," reading him like an hourglass with the sand running out. And Jim, far out of my reach in a morphine haze, losing speech because of the tumors pressing on his spine, relentlessly taking away all strength and feeling in his legs, his trunk, moving upwards toward his arms and head.

An owl hoots twice up on the hill above the river. What will hold me, here and now, in this moment on the edge of nothing?

Last spring, I woke suddenly at dawn, feeling a presence in our room. Still half-asleep, I nevertheless instantly felt there were angels. I wanted to cry—not from sorrow, but from awe. Jim was still asleep, curled on his side away from me towards the big, peaked window that looks down on the river below. I moved in close behind him, inhaling the sweet smell of his soft brown hair, and thought of waking him to tell him that perhaps we weren't going to be doing this hard journey alone. But the experience was so utterly new to me—a surprising moment of grace in early morning light—that I said nothing.

We'd already spent nearly a year in breathless suspense, wondering if the single, large mole on his back had sent its poison into Jim's blood and nerves. It all began with a casual conversation in the bathroom. I must have sensed something dark and imminent to have suddenly said without forethought, "I think I'm going to see a dermatologist and have my annual skin check."

"I should go too," said Jim then, "my mole has been itching."

I took a look and suddenly could not breathe. Two days later, it was the way the dermatologist hurried to get the mole off Jim's back that had me bent over with ringing in my ears. "Go to Texas," the doctor advised us, "that's where the best research is being done."

But when Jim heard about the mole, his first response was not about how to fight for life, but how to prepare for death. All we heard from the doctor was what he didn't say, but what we heard in his voice: melanoma was deadly. Jim's grandfather had died of melanoma, we knew that much. We floundered, indecisive, while trying to create inner stability with a larger spiritual perspective. We were two idealistic, basically healthy, rather impoverished teachers who had had little experience with conventional medicine. We were, like many children of the Sixties, "spiritual but not religious." Which left us swimming in circles since we'd never found solid ground to support us.

After the diagnosis, I began praying aloud, my own made-up prayer, each night before bed: "Infinite Spirit, Creative Spirit, Light. Love. Life. Help us to know that Jim is whole in every part of his being. Help us to be strong, Help us to be clear."

I prayed without the sense that I deserved to be heard. I prayed like a bad child who saw it was time to be good but who still nursed a seed of resentment because she couldn't manage on her own terms. Argued too: "When I ask you for help, God, I want to be clear that you're not the same God who sends people to war. You're not the one who decrees that women are servants to men, and who punishes, judges, and destroys."

It was a prayer crafted with Sixties-generation ambivalence, a mishmash of half-tested convictions, plus a bit of shyness, awkwardness, and hope.

This is not to say that we were not seekers—Steiner's anthroposophy was the territory we had been searching for guidance. It was about to become a defining light for the journey ahead.

If Jim prayed, he did not tell me, and I felt it wrong to ask because he had withdrawn deeply into himself. His father, who had died when Jim was in his twenties, had come to him in a dream, sat for a moment next to him on the bed, then faded away. Did this mean "I'm waiting for you, don't worry?" we wondered together.

There was that conversation before we married, a prenuptial warning: "I've always felt," Jim had told me, "that someday I will have to face something very powerful and difficult in my life, and afterwards, I will either be dead or I will become a monk."

That was when Jim turned thirty-eight. Now he's forty-eight and so am I. Someday looms like tomorrow.

My mother, a grounded, robustly healthy woman, had to put her head down during our wedding, and wondered afterwards why. However much she approved of my marrying again after a painful divorce, witnessing my act of commitment seemed to have made her suddenly dizzy and afraid, she told me.

And what will happen to me? I'd wondered to myself when I'd first heard Jim's dark prediction. "May the events which seek me come unto me," went an old verse about destiny and acceptance that I'd encountered in school. If I believed this, my heart could say that I would honor Jim's deep sense of his life path, apart from mine. My heart said we were not bound by time and would go on forever.

But my head said nothing bad could possibly happen to us and time was real and here and now, and we deserved the same amount of it as anyone else.

There was also that early morning talk about paralysis, long before we even knew Jim was ill. We were still in the wonder of discovery in our relationship, revealing our most secret dreams and fears: "If that ever happened to me, I wouldn't want you to have to take care of me," he said.

"Of course, I would care for you," I said. "It would be my joy to do that." We changed the subject, felt awkward, reached for one another.

But why no talk about me?

6

Tonight, out here in so many kinds of darkness, a single light and Jim in the distance, I feel myself crack into two pieces: an old self caught up in fear, grief, resistance, and helplessness, another self tentatively testing new ground with the smallest, humblest sense of awe.

The State of Vermont permits "taking care of your own" from the moment of death to burial in your own backyard if you have space. I have promised Jim that no stranger's hand will ever touch him. But I'm of a generation raised in abstractions. My grandmothers, my mother too, knew the metallic smell of passages, the steamy odor of lye and ashes, the diminishing warmth inside a fresh-killed chicken and the way to watch for a fever to turn. They knew about doing things because you have no choice, because you accept the life you've been given.

I don't want the look of grim endurance I've seen in some dark, curling photographs. Some of that look may be there, but also a hope for some transparency, like in the eyes of the newly born, both innocence and wonder.

How? How will I give Jim my best self, be his steadfast companion right to the edge of the abyss and not cling when he steps off?

I'm standing now by the pond and the moon, slipping out from behind a cloud, shines down into the black water like an answer.

Somewhere I hear a voice saying, "Just fill him up with love, that's all."

7

GALLERY

Jim's watercolor of waves breaking on white sand. I see him, he sees me.

Jim's ponytail and the wool hat he knit for himself all festooned with feathers.

Jim as a statue, posing on a London park bench.

Jim flirting, one eyebrow up and the other down.

Jim's dark eyes: a look that pierces, one that dreams.

Jim's hand taking mine, leading through the dark to a night in his English cottage.

Jim's hair then, curling in that gentle place behind his ear.

Jim's square hands with big bumps at the base of the thumbs.

Jim's feet with high arches, and his comment that he's never fully come down to earth.

Jim's mission: architecture must inspire people to self-knowledge, inner freedom.

Jim's cosmic dream: each finger connects with an invisible, silvery thread to the stars.

Jim rocking out to Elvis while he cooks me dinner.

Jim joking, "One of us is not necessary here," after we voice identical thoughts.

Jim in ecstasy with a visitor's baby zonked out on his chest.

Jim's made-up story about a little boy who saves a great whale.

Jim enchanting children in our shared kindergarten class.

Jim shaping our garden beds into a dancing woman, her head crowned by roses.

Jim and lovemaking, in the garden, on the porch, on the island in the middle of the river.

The wonder of Jim loving me.

SLIDESHOW

Nite Charm for Jim

Green mist
Go
Fly sparkling silver
go and help him
go and care for him
a small hope far inside
twinkles like a star
if you walk the lonely road
it may not be so far
—from Mary, age seven

9.11.93

A month since the doctor sent Jim home to die. Jim wakes from a dream and struggles for words: "I'm going somewhere. I don't know where."

9.13

Jim (as I help him sit up): "You're causing me pain but I love you anyway."

9.15

Me (sobbing): "Can't you say anything? I'm losing you."

Jim (making a great effort at word-finding): "You mean you want me to confirm you?"

Me (crying harder): "Oh, yes!"

He reaches up and gently touches my hair, my face. Looks at me so intently. As if memorizing.

9.28

The home health nurse: "Keep the catheter clean with soap and water. Try to get him on his side regularly. Move his limbs around three times a day. Make a schedule to help you remember everything."

6:00 AM: 1 morphine, long acting

7:00 AM: 1 morphine, 1 oxycontin

11:00 AM: 1 oxycontin (some pain midmorning)

4:00 PM: 2 morphine (more pain)

7:00 PM: 2 oxycontin, 2 stool softeners

Pain until 10:30 PM. Then he sleeps.

9.29

Dear Rondi,

I will continue to pray for you both and have considered coming to see you. While I was doing this, I had a curious dream: I dreamt that I was there and Jim was dead and all the family was sitting in the living room and you were off in the bedroom. While I was sitting there, there appeared a small figure on a wide bookshelf above my head. It was a beautiful boy about two feet high or so, about nine years old, with dark brown hair. He looked, I suppose, as Jim might have looked at that age. He was peering over the edge of the shelf as into an abyss, afraid to jump. Whereas I saw him, he seemed instead to see a void of the unknown.

I stood up and caught him as he jumped, saying, "Here is Jim's soul; Rondi will want this." You came out of the bedroom and I gave the boy to you and you took him away with you. After some time, you came back with the boy much transformed. He was plump, smiling, dressed in a blue bathrobe, and wearing spectacles. You took him over to where Jim's body was lying on the couch and Jim sat up to take the boy-soul and was fine again.

Our love and prayers are with you.

Your sister,

Kristin

9.30

Jim sleeps deeply, coughing heavily when he wakes. His tailbone looks red. Maybe a blister and bedsores are starting? I massage his back and stretch his arms, too much. He has little strength left and it's easy to hurt him. My tension hurts him. My fears hurt him. I can't give him anything simple.

10.1

Jim is more conscious this morning and seems depressed. I only give him one oxycontin and two tablespoons of milk of magnesia. He refuses to take the steroids and Dilantin. He's angry, wants no drugs in his system.

Afraid of a seizure, I mash up the pills in yogurt. He throws them up, defiant.

I turn him on his side and our neighbor L. is at the door to offer a massage. She touches him so attentively, as if listening for a response in each cell, shifting his body as it asks to be shifted, holding him with such reverence. I struggle to be grateful that she can touch him, giving him ease, feeling that I cannot.

10.3

Severe intestinal cramping, and then he's weak and exhausted. I move him to bed. He falls asleep on his side and sleeps all day. When he wakes, he eats some supper: mashed potatoes, green beans, chicken. For the first time in a week, he asks to brush his teeth before bed. He has a restless, wakeful night, but no real discomfort.

10.4

He's wide awake and wants a big glass of orange juice. Food is hope. *Will I ever nourish him enough now?* Food is life. Food means he's staying.

10.6

Severe head pain, retching, abdominal pain. I give him two Tylenol tablets and lots of water. He is still refusing to increase his drugs. He hasn't eaten for two days.

10.7

Severe head pain. Jim vomits a small amount of greenish fluid.

Seizure. His left hand is weak, the left side of his face contracted.

L. comes again with her knowledge of care for a body in pain. She's tall and graceful, and the spicy smell of fall comes through the door with her. She shows me how to hold Jim's head so gently, being present, with intention.

What's my intent? Everything I've longed to do for Jim for these past months flows through my hands. L. gives me hope, so today I keep it simple, keep myself listening, stop pushing him with my anxiety and grief. I just stand there at the head of the bed, cradle his head, and open my heart.

Now, I feel my hands full of prickles, electric. *So, this is what pain feels like? I can feel something invisible?*

The sensation stops. My hands feel cool. I find myself sighing deeply. Jim is asleep and peaceful. I sit down by his bed in amazement. There's more to this world, to each of us, than I have realized.

I can know something invisible.

10.8

Jim (struggling to talk to me as he wakes):

"I hadn't realized I'd gone through the door.

"I'm just realizing about the date. My date.

"Tourist, tourist! Travel? Yes. Go to the feast."

Jim's tumors are pressing on the part of his brain that controls speech. I know that he's saying, "I'm really leaving, I just figured it out."

How can I confirm this to him, to myself? Anguish leaves me speechless.

10.9

I'm dressed as a bride. I can't get it together to go the wedding. The cake is on the floor. The bouquet lies on the cake.

When I wake up, I write down the dream in an old notebook and begin to make a record. There are two mes now talking to one another through pen and paper.

Later in the day, Dr. H. visits: "You're at a fork in the road."

"It's going to get harder," he's saying.

10.10

Ed B. comes to sleep next to Jim and, for the first time in weeks, I am willing to step back.

"Just fill him up with love, that's all."

I'm giddy in the moonlight, a big, open space in my throat.

10.10

Mammy comes. Jim's face floods with relief at the sight of his mother, because he knows she will punch out anyone and anything that threatens her son. Maybe this cancer thing too.

She will stay and help for as long as it takes, Mammy tells me. She's already tutored in loss: a husband, brothers, sisters, parents, friends. "Just keep walking," she says to me.

When she massages the legs of her beloved only son, I can hear her silent, keening prayer: *Take me, oh please, take me instead.*

10.11

Dr. L. calls, shocked to hear the news. Tears when I hear her voice, although I've always been a bit intimidated by her. Born in South Africa and imposingly Dutch, like my somewhat stern grandmother, there is also humor and warmth. She lives two hours away in a home and clinic Jim designed for her and her medical practice. Her treatment follows the principles of anthroposophical medicine. Jim is not a collection of dire symptoms to treat, but an individual with a threefold nature, body and soul and spirit. His care will be about maintaining a balance among the three aspects to minimize pain and to prepare his soul for the great challenge of leaving his body.

Dr. L.'s friendship is ground we can trust. She will show us how to support Jim's decision to give up the morphine protocol prescribed by his original doctor. She'll coach me in the old ways: the poultices and compresses, the massages and herbal remedies, the simple knowledge and work of women who have done the loving management of birthing and dying for centuries.

She comes to the house, stops inside the door, and looks around at the chaos in the living room: Jim on the foldout couch (because our bedroom is upstairs), the wheelchair, the commode, and the piles of blankets, sweaters, swabs, dressings, medicines, notes, papers, and towels.

"There is no support here for Jim's soul," she says.

We clean the room and order is restored. An adjustable hospital bed is rented and a table with flowers placed nearby. No signs of chaotic dissolution here any longer, just peace and beauty. Food arranged with care on a tray, with beauty. Quiet voices, gentle touch. Beauty. No frantic signs of attempts to negate the inevitable. Acceptance, with beauty.

WEAR BIG SHOES

*"The experience of dying as a conscious, creative act
has become a focus of interest in recent times
as people are more and more recognizing it as the
final, culminating act of life itself, the crowning event
for which one's whole life has been a preparation."*
—Michael Gellert

Dr. L.'s care for the dying, based on the philosophy of Rudolf
Steiner:

1. Detoxify the body through sweat and warmth: Use
   equisetum (horsetail grass) poultices to stimulate kidney
   function; coffee and chamomile enemas to regulate the
   bowels.

2. Stimulate bodily processes with hot packs of *millefolium*
   (yarrow) or castor oil on the abdomen.

3. Stimulation will keep him self-aware until the end. If his
   ego detaches, there will be more pain.

4. Reduce or eliminate morphine if desired. If possible,
   substitute with homeopathic remedies for nerve pain.

5. Massage and bathe him daily. Massage his feet at night to keep him fully integrated in his body. His ego will need support for facing the moment of death.

6. Certain homeopathic remedies, like gold, will provide emotional strength.

"You can do this, Rondi," Dr. L. says.

Like a pioneer woman? I think. *Am I that strong?*

For Jim, fierce love.

10.12

Dr. L. leaves. For the first time in nearly two months the house feels peaceful and in order. Jim is sleeping after his morning bath. The clock ticks out the time to practice eternity and the sun shafts through the open window and deepens the silence in the room. I can finally hear the river singing.

I sit down with Mammy. "I will nurse him until the end. We will wash his body and keep it here in ceremony for three days and three nights. Then we will take it to the crematorium. Our hands alone will be the last to touch him," I say.

It's not her way, but Mammy gives me, the woman her son chose, the greatest gift: her unequivocal yes.

10.13

Life has settled into routine and now I think it will stay like this and I will be able to breathe. I suddenly long to be out in the autumn fires. Mammy nods okay and I tell Jim I'm going out.

I drive back into the hills, following unnamed dirt roads overhung with blazing maples, absorbing the vivid contrasts against the deep emerald of the fields, still free from frost. As I drive, my awareness of the autumn that will always be, and is Jim's last, begins to clog my throat with tears. I head towards home, weeping, and as the car tops a rise and heads down a long hill, the tears stop.

I can see Jim. He's in his red wool shirt in the distance, down near the bottom of the road, arms swinging in his familiar, bouncing walk, head down. The closer I get, the more I know it's Jim, and he's done the same as I, just taken a break, left that sad house and is out for a walk in the crisp fall air.

The car draws near. I begin to pull up, to exclaim with amazement, and then, with a flash, Jim is gone and a stranger is in his place, looking at me with curiosity as I peer out at him and then speed away.

10.14

Dr. L.'s protocol makes a shape of sanity in our days. *I can do this, just make this my life now,* I think. It's a relief to live with such simple purpose, tending, nurturing, gentling.

But things refuse to stay the same. Jim is in pain all night, much moaning. His head is very hot at the back of his neck. I offer morphine, but he refuses. He has little ability to speak, but seems to be determined to do without the medication.

3:30 AM: I dream a poem for us.

Open yourself to love now. Go.
Go to yourself in silence.
Wear Big Shoes.

I'm writing all of this down. I can't seem to pray, because I'm too busy watching this other woman in her play, wondering why the words of her script are not as wise and deep like in the movies, telling her to keep moving, while reminding her to record these moments of unexpected awe, revelation, coded truths that might show her later how to survive the silence.

10.15

I see Jim walking around the house. He is dressed in a blue corduroy shirt, which hangs out over his old khaki shorts. His legs are strong and hairy above his white socks and hiking boots. A navy blue bandanna is knotted on his head and I can only see the side of his face and his chin-length brown hair (like when we first met).

How he can be dressed and walking around when he is supposed to be in bed dying of cancer?

I follow Jim into the bathroom. The sink is next to the window, a tub behind. Over in a corner next to the sink on the left, there is someone, a young girl, playing with blocks. (Is that another me, so innocent and unconcerned, constructing a tower of days to come?)

Jim goes to the sink and looks at his reflection in the mirror. He says to himself, "I feel that I am on the edge of something very mysterious."

I reach for him, turn him around, beg for a hug. He gives me a wonderful, warm, full-body one, then kisses me on the lips. "I'm going to build you a house in the clouds," he says.

I sit down on the edge of the tub in our half-sheet-rocked bathroom in our half-renovated house and look up at him with a grin: "Okay. But this time I'm not coming until it's finished," I joke.

10.15

The children from our kindergarten class have suddenly appeared outside and are running around on the lawn by the river. I watch them through our big windows, but I'm frozen in place and cannot find my way to them. They seem almost unreal—as if I'm watching a movie of a past life. Some squat or kneel and, with the help of their parents, carefully plant daffodils in the grass. A promise for me in the spring. Two pots of soup are left on the doorstep.

10.18

My sister Andrea arrives with angel message cards, little pieces of stiff paper with watercolor cartoon images of angels on them. On each card there is a single word in calligraphy. I throw the cards in a pile on the floor and pick one. *Courage*, it says to me. I sigh deeply, and feel suddenly less alone. I'm in a slow dance with an invisible, inevitable force.

Is it about love? Is it about fear? A single word, unanticipated, unpredictable, yet mirroring the mystery I'm caught in, suggests I can learn, even know, be called to a better self, while I muddle through.

10.20

Jim and I are in town in the red car. Jim gets out, to my great surprise, and goes over to a group of children climbing in some trees. He begins to play with them. I am amazed; this is the first time he has decided to walk in months. I let him alone with the children and run into L. and C. We get caught up in a conversation about how to help Jim maintain this new state.

All of a sudden, I realize I have forgotten to keep track of Jim's needs and I've lost him. I run through the streets of the town looking everywhere for him, skating and sliding about on the soles of my shoes. (I can't get a grip?) I'm filled with guilt and dread, looking everywhere, in the windows of stores, some of which have closed for the night. I finally go back to the car and Jim is already inside, lying down and looking worn out. I run over, crying with relief, angry with myself for not realizing he would be there. I throw my arms around him.

PENDULUM

"Research: The dying person will need, when he has crossed the threshold, all the strength of selfhood which he has gathered in the process of facing the great change of death knowingly. . . Without the body, the self has to establish another means of self-consciousness. The moment of death, clearly known, can act as a beacon illuminating the consciousness of being a self, long after the time has passed."

—*Evelyn Francis Capel*

10.22

Strength. Peace. Love, the angels say.

10.24

Jim (with great effort at word finding): "Maybe we should get a few people to spread the word."

Me: "What word? My word or yours?"

Jim (looking sly): "It's a secret. Sort of about me."

I play dumb, knowing that he's talking about letting people know he's dying, but again I lack the courage to respond. I can speak better through my hands, but my voice just won't come out, cannot acknowledge the truth, even now.

10.25

Jim has asked my brother to take him to a river and leave him there. I am sure Jim has gone to jump in. I frantically dial the phone, but can't get through or dial correctly. I'm sobbing wildly.

10.26

Jim insists on getting up. His legs collapse under him and he crashes to the floor. We put him in the back seat of a long, black, shiny car with black windows. N. wants to take him on a walk to a special place in the woods. I am angry because he doesn't realize that Jim can't walk. Meanwhile, I am carefully smoothing and spreading a cloth on top of the car in order to put flowers and candles on it.

10.27

Dr. L. comes again to check on us and hands me a pendulum made of brass. I wrap its chain around my fingers and feel the weight of it dragging at my hand. She shows me how to use it as a divination tool to help me make choices about Jim's care.

She advises me that deep down, my whole self knows what strengthens me—which entails facing or finding the truth in my situation. Yet my fear and confusion cause me to second-guess myself constantly—and this is weakening my ability to cope.

The lesson: Despite the disordered jumble in my head, the rest of me is a being with greater awareness who knows and responds to what is right for us and what wastes time and energy.

I program the shining, spinning pendulum to be my translator. A spin to the right is my *Yes, strength*. To the left, my *No, weakness*.

Everything has become hidden: my life as I knew it, my future as I dreamed it, Jim's final days, the insidiously slow creep of death's date toward us. My body can perhaps show me the truth. Somewhere in the blankness, there are messages: Trust? *Yes.* Deny? *No.* Release? *Yes.*

The angels are here too, the quiet, powerful presence that appeared in our bedroom six months ago which I am now grateful to accept.

"Is Jim going to die?" I finally ask. And then, suddenly, I feel a great inner release, like a deep sigh. *It's okay. Let go. It's going to be okay.*

10.28

Our backyard has a huge apple tree in it. The apples are the size of grapefruits and need to be picked. I crawl under the branches to look at the trunk and notice it has a very sensual, powerful feeling about it. There is an open space under the trunk, and the bottom of the tree curves above it like a pubic bone. Everything feels pregnant and moist. I pick the apples; they look so healthy on the outside, but inside they are soft and beginning to rot.

As I write down the dream, I realize I have my period. I'm angry that my body won't free me of its animal ways, reminding me, cruelly, that I can make more life, even now.

10.29

Jim has an appetite! Bacon and eggs! We offer him Mozart, Beethoven, Bach. Music to die by: celestially inspired notes for constructing a ladder to heaven. He wants none of it, no dramatic sendoff. The least sound causes torment. "Just let me be," he seems to be saying.

10.30

Jim welcomes a kiss for the first time in more than a month. He's fully present and swaggers and makes a funny face when propped up like a king on pillows. Expresses concern for my well-being: "No, finish eating before you take care of me."

Me, selfishly complaining about a body ache, wanting his attention.

Jim: "I'll trade ya."

His appetite is much improved. Right arm nearly useless, all pins and needles. He can still move his fingers. Neck, shoulder, and back pain, but not so bad as to suggest a need for morphine. Gut not bothering him much, and he's much more clear, conscious. Dr. L.'s treatments seem to be helping.

Jim's face is shining, his skin pink and glowing. He wears a lavishly embroidered hat on his now-bald head. Sometimes I want just to stand and look at him. As his body shrinks, somehow my sense of him expands.

11.1

A hard night. Jim has intense pain in his neck and shoulder. Lovingly, "You're a wild, reckless woman," when I hurt him as I adjust his pillows.

11.2

During Jim's bath, I notice his teeth are chattering. By evening, his head is hot and he has disappeared.

CROSSROADS

Research: Wash the body. Pack the rectum with gauze.
Close the eyes and tie the mouth closed. Dress the
body and after it is in the coffin, pack ice around it,
between the arms and torso, legs and on belly and
chest if you are keeping it at home for a period of time
before burial. Renew ice every twelve hours.

11.3

On the phone, Dr. L. advises we apply lemon wraps, old wives' medicine from Europe, to reduce the fever of Jim's pneumonia. "Cut a lemon in half in body-temperature water," she says. "Score each half into fourths. Press the cut halves down into the water to release their juice. Soak long cotton wraps in this solution and squeeze them out. Wrap the cloths around his legs and cover them with a towel. Renew the moisture as needed."

Jim's fever soars to 105 degrees. His eyes are clouded and strange. But after two hours, the fever goes down.

11.6

Dr. L.: "This condition will go on for about seven days, and then he'll be at a crossroads. He may go, or the tumors may go, because, during the burning of a fever, tumors are not growing."

11.7

Dr. L.: "Twenty-four hours before he dies, his guardian angel will leave to wait for him at the threshold between this world and the spiritual worlds. And you will notice a change. His face will darken. He could be more awake, perhaps restless, or suddenly in a coma."

"At the moment his spirit leaves his body, he will feel as though he is going down a long tunnel," she says. "Place lighted candles to the right and left of him so that he sees the light as he draws away."

After I put the phone down, I blindly reach for the angel cards:

Trust. Courage. Peace. Love. Tenderness, the angels say.

11.8

Jim is very near to death. Doctors, undertakers, Jim's physiotherapist, all men, are working over him as he lies on a stretcher. He takes his last breath. I have been held back somehow and have not been able to share that moment with him. One of the men is blocking my view.

I hear someone say that Jim has died. I go into a constant, contorted kind of crying, a deep, throaty bleating that is forced out from the center of my gut. While I do this, I explain to my mother, who is standing nearby, that I'm okay, that I just need to make this sound for a while.

Jim is dumped into a narrow coffin and put in the back of a van. I catch a view of his body as they're lifting him. It is still pink. I see his face in the coffin; it is very slack, all the skin loose, his head to one side, no dignity or preparation.

I explain to the men, between sobs, that Mammy and I are supposed to be taking care of him. They put him back in the room, but everything is wrong. There is no table for the coffin; the pedestal is too high.

The house fills with strangers: repairmen, a neighbor who comes to sit in a corner and knit, some young people who have radios or a TV on. I try to make everyone be quiet and go away. They are not very responsive, but at least the TV is shut off. The repairmen persist in working on a lower part of the wall right next to where Jim's body is lying. I tell them loudly and not very nicely to go away.

I find Mammy and try to get a sense of whether she is going to help with Jim. She equivocates, and then starts washing his body. I can't seem to be able to, things get in the way. I'm still bleating.

Finally, I help move Jim. As I do, he pats my back in a sympathetic, loving way and moans. I exclaim, "I thought you were dead! Aren't you?"

"I don't know," he replies, "I think I am." He is making all kinds of noises, groans, as he is being moved. It is very *troubling, as if he is still in his body. Mammy is doing all of the tending and I don't seem to be able to. I'm seeing the opportunity of helping Jim die with grace and beauty out of control and out of my hands. Someone is giving Mammy instructions about what to do. She is looking in the top of Jim's skull, which is empty and clean, and saying, "So, when I put the dirt in there, I dry it first," and whoever is directing her agrees. It's as though Jim is being taken apart in pieces and he's still pink, still sounding alive, even though he looks dead.*

I can't do anything except bleat helplessly in the chaos.

I wake sobbing.

11.9

There is a wooden tower that has recently appeared, a small space supported by four legs that are spread like on the Eiffel Tower. Lashed to the legs are crosspieces, mounted close together for climbing. At the top, in the Tower, there is something that has never been seen before, something spectacular, like the discovery of color.

Everyone in the neighborhood is climbing up to behold this marvel. Everyone in my family is there, and I am urged to join the crowd, especially by Dad, who has come back from the dead to support me.

I hang back because of grief; I don't want to be "entertained." But finally, I go to the base of the ladder and I'm the last in line. Dad, who died seven years ago, shepherds me up, eager for me to see what is there. I climb into the small room at the top. It is full of strange and exotic flowers in vibrant colors. There are masses of cerulean blue ones and I decide I like them best. There are also others that are blood red.

I am impressed, but unwilling to let go of my sorrow. If this is a preview visit to heaven, I'm not ready for it. I climb down and head home without waiting or telling anyone (especially Dad) where I am going or why I'm not staying around.

The terrain I pass through on the way back to Jim is stony with gray-green grass, clipped short. It feels like cemetery ground.

11.10

The home health nurse is amazed to see how clear eyed and present Jim appears, despite the high fevers that rage through the nights. He smiles and is able to joke with her this morning. He shines; his skin glows pink from all of the detoxifying and massage from Dr. L.'s treatment. Privately, the nurse tells me that the general health and appearance of Jim's body suggests that he is not close to death, because there are no signs of degradation.

She leaves, and two hours later, Jim is burning again, burning out of his body, another night of leg wraps and holding. He is having trouble breathing.

Dr. L. says yes, there can be an oxygen tent and antibiotics and heroic attempts to keep him from leaving. Or there can be simple loving and support while he finds his own way to let go.

Jim can't tell me what to do. I choose to let *It* be.

11.11

The tension that has been building for weeks breaks as Mammy and I have a big fight in the back room, away from Jim. She can't bear that people are talking to Jim about his impending death. I now want the conversation out in the open so that we can say goodbye. Two champions for Jim's soul, and because we love him, we're both right.

Even though Jim is in the other room, he feels the strife. Even though he has been without speech for weeks, he calls out for me and makes it stop.

In the evening, his face is dark. Something is different.

Mammy and her sister V. take the first shift. I say goodnight to Jim, telling him that I will be back at 4 AM.

Around 1 AM, Jim asks his mother to feed him Cheerios. *A gift for her,* I think later. She gave him his first and now his last meal.

A LIGHT IN THE WINDOW

Dear rondi.
to let go is not sad for
the Person but only sad for the
PeoPle who are left behind.
Its sad but there not rely dead. there just
beyond the next mountun
beyond the next hill. so
don't feel sad
baucus even thoe you
cant see him he is there.
Lots of love
—Lila XXXO, age seven

11.12, 4 AM

I am alone with Jim in the dimly lit room when his labored breathing, which has filled the house for a week with its harshness, abruptly ceases. I put my hand on his chest, querying and knowing all at once. "Jim?"

Shaken, I awkwardly light the candles on either side of the head of the bed, feeling him pulling away. It's like leaving a light in the window to tell him I'm keeping watch, always.

I call Mom, Mammy, and her sister V. and we stand around the bed while Jim's heartbeat grows fainter and fainter and finally stops. He just slips away.

Silence.

I begin to sob, with grief, relief, my face against his, thinking, *You did it, Jim.*

Mammy is afraid I will call him back, warns me not to beg him to stay. Her old family tradition says to be sure not to cling, but to make the passage easy.

I won't call, I won't. But I've held myself together for so long. I need my tears now to help me to accept, to finally, at last, let him go.

Outside, in the early morning dark, there is a sudden rush of wind against the house, and then rain.

HEARTSEASE

"I woke around 5 AM, thinking I had heard a wolf's howl.
I thought immediately of Jim, but wondered, Why the wolf?
Then I remembered that my name is Lups. Lupus. Wolf."
–Dr. L.

9 AM

We wash and tend Jim's body, his mother and I, just as we have every other darkening autumn day. And even though his body has been nothing before but fragile bones and huge hands and slender feet, it was full of him. Now it is empty.

I dress Jim in the brown, handwoven cotton caftan that I made for him as a present before we married. My mother, Mammy, other family, friends, and I lift him and put him in the simple pine coffin that my son Marcus helped make for him. I cradle his head, Mammy his feet. She remarks afterward that she was amazed at their beauty.

I place two small flat stones on Jim's eyelids. His eyes stay closed without them, but I am fussing, in a strange, detached sort of way, about making it right. His mouth is slack, but closed, so I don't tie it as otherwise instructed in my reading.

Nothing is real. I feel as though I have entered one of my dreams. I go out to the garden, which is luminous in the post-rain morning light. Everything is November brown except for some cheerful yellow, blue, and purple Johnny Jump-ups—also known as Heartsease—that are still blooming in straggling profusion. I pick a big bouquet and go back to the house.

I put the flowers in Jim's hands. In his long brown robe, he looks like an ancient saint.

T. brings the dry ice. He packs it around the body. Jim was too private a person to want his body on view. After a long stretch of silence, we close the lid and take turns, sharing the screwdriver, putting in the screws.

It's Mammy's turn. She shakes her head decisively: NO.

A ROOM FULL OF STARS

"In eternal time, all is now; time is presence."
–John O'Donohue

11.12, noon

T. and D. arrive with billows of autumn flowers. *A time to love and hate such beauty,* I think. We are beginning the ancient tradition of holding a vigil for three days and three nights with Jim's body. T. sits down next to Jim's coffin and begins to read silently from the Book of John in the Bible. She will be a point of rest and attention for us, a single person thinking only of Jim while others deal with distractions. After T., others will come and take turns sitting next to Jim, all day, all night, for the next seventy-two hours.

I arrange a cloth, a picture of Jim, the flowers, and some candles on top of the coffin. More lit candles are placed everywhere, in every window, on every surface. These will burn day and night until we are finished with our goodbyes. The room fills with their sweet, waxy fragrance. I put out a book for our kindergarten children to draw in when they come, and a guest book for grownups.

43

It's all happening too fast. The structures of mourning in community eclipse my ability to fully take in what has just occurred in our home, in my life.

All day, the house is full of people. When the children come, I take each one on my lap and describe how beautiful and peaceful Jim is lying inside the golden pine box in his brown robe, holding flowers. There are lots of children sitting now on the floor next to the coffin, busily drawing with crayons, making pictures for me and Jim.

Six-year-old Bridget's picture: Jim is lying on top of a bier in his brown robe. His head, outlined in green crayon, is turned sideways to give a frozen crayon grimace. He's really dead. But above his prone body, a dancing, smiling spirit in a purple robe has emerged from his heart and is floating joyfully upwards.

An enormous angel with rainbow wings takes up the whole top of the page, while streaming an extra rainbow down to frame the scene. A blue stripe across the top of the page is sky.

On the back of the picture, Bridget writes:

Jim: I lve you eevin if
you are in havin

When evening comes, the candles fill the room with soft, golden light and are reflected in every window. The room is full of stars.

E. touches me on the arm and offers to give me a massage. We go upstairs and I lie down. As she rubs oil on my body, I can't feel me. I feel Jim's body. The everyday ritual of touching him is deeply imprinted, the only tangible piece of him that remains.

It seems that I don't have a body anymore. Jim and I made one body between us, where we read each other's thoughts with one mind, loved with one heart. We lived in that body, not the one that hangs on me now. *What will I do with this strange, empty shape?*

11.13

Friends, school parents, and family are taking turns keeping watch by the coffin. And the hours pass, all day, all night, in candlelight or shafts of sun, with the sound of the river when the door opens and people come and go. The house is otherwise sealed off from the world by the power of ceremony and witness. We are waiting for something to complete itself, for Jim, for all of us. Three days, three nights, and our lives will begin again, move forward without him.

Late in the second day, I ask to be alone and sit by myself next to the coffin. Feelings of inadequacy begin to creep in, as if, rather than just being, I have to start doing again, to continue my job as a healer and fixer, to make sure everything is cleaned up, taken care of, smoothed out, checking for more possible failures. Easier to go there than to feel the hollow space where

Jim used to be. But each time my mind searches for *What Now* and *If Only*, a press of reassurance flows into me. *Let Go.*

The doing part seems to be taking place in other worlds and it's not my job anymore to fix anything. My understanding of the whole—the passage and power of Jim through my life—will come later and there will be time then.

A whole new country of time.

11.15

Seventy-two hours after Jim leaves, family and a few friends gather near the coffin. We say a few words, sing "Amazing Grace" in tight, trembling voices. It is a soft, cool, misty morning without a breath of air, still half-dark at 6:00 AM in November. Outside, the trees are dark and wet; the unmown grass is still green, looking like humps of moss. The icy gray river shushes and mumbles. I seem to hear voices inside it, intimate, the way you can hear your neighbors conversing nearby on a quiet summer day.

Four of us carry Jim in his coffin out of the house, across the grass next to the river and then through the heart of our garden with its beds shaped so the whole looks like a dancing figure. Our procession is marked by the flickering light of our candles. The Jim we now bear seems to have slipped into another age, perhaps one where he would have felt more himself in his brown woven robe, his hands full of blue, yellow, and purple heartsease flowers.

We put his coffin in a van and will drive it an hour across the mountains to a crematorium in western Vermont. Candles are left behind, still burning, on top of the stone cover of the well. When we return three hours later, tiny flames are still wavering in thick puddles of wax and not a breath of air has snuffed them out. Nothing has moved here; everything still held outside of time.

Later, I find that Jim's watch has stopped as well.

Family and friends enter the house to restore it to its former state. I beg to be alone. I have not been by myself for any significant period for four months.

While Jim's body is disappearing into ash and bone an hour away, I head down to a wild place by the river, out of sight from the house and the concerns of family and friends. As I come to the edge of the water, I hear nothing but relentless noise.

Something breaks loose inside.

WHAT HAPPENED TO JIM?

Skeptics: He had a comforting hallucination of going down a long tunnel. Then he disappeared into nothingness.

Near-death researchers, survivors, believers: He left his body, went down a long tunnel toward a brilliant white light, met a high spiritual being, and experienced great peace and contact with loved ones on the Other Side.

Catholics: He left his body and went through judgment, and then to heaven, purgatory, or hell, depending on his capacity for purification.

Conservative Protestants: He went into oblivion until the Last Judgment.

Moderate Protestants: He went immediately to heaven and reunited with his loved ones, or to hell for everlasting suffering.

Liberal Protestants: He remained conscious and capable of interacting with the living. If he lived a bad life, he would learn to recognize his misdeeds, but there is no hell and eternal suffering.

Jews: His body is tended with ritual and care. After he completely detaches from his physical body (which takes up to a year), he will go through a period of purification, also for twelve months and then be sent down to earth help others. The righteous may be resurrected to enjoy a second life in a physical realm that will exist at the end of days after the Messiah has come.

Buddhists: At death, his consciousness (humans have no fixed entity like a soul) had a blinding experience of true reality. If he was too distracted by his old habits to be able to recognize it, he'll be born again in another form, in another lifetime, until he reaches enlightenment.

Muslims: He will live on in another kind of existence until resurrection on a day of judgment, when God will punish him if he has not lived a moral life.

Hindus: He will experience a blissful, light-filled transition from one state to another and go to the next world to experience the results of his deeds on earth. Then, unless he has eradicated all desire, he will be reborn in a different body, through reincarnation.

Anthroposophists: He entered an unknown world and felt lost without his body. Hearing the prayers and good thoughts of those on earth helped him stay connected with his ego-consciousness, while with his guardian angel, he went through a direct, living experience of each of his deeds on earth, including how his choices affected others. After several states and levels of spiritual education, he will either remain in the spiritual world or be reincarnated so that he can continue to experience whatever he needs to learn.

WHERE IS THE LAND OF THE DEAD?

"We have falsely spatialized the Eternal world and made out in some kind of dream that it is a way out beyond the furthest galaxy, when in fact the eternal world isn't a place like that at all, but it's actually a different state of being. So that the soul of the person goes no place, because there's no place to go."
—John O'Donohue

How can Jim be gone when I have only to pick up his shirt and his smell fills my senses, like a translation between spirit and matter?

How can Jim be gone when I have only to ask, and my mouth still knows how he tastes?

How can Jim be gone when I have only to think of his voice and every cell in my body begins to vibrate?

How can Jim be gone when I can close my eyes and see every detail of his body?

In between the worlds, Jim and I are standing, looking at one another, asking how could we not *be?*

My senses, still knowing their best work, make the afterimage.

Afterglow.

In the background of my Self, burning.

In a somewhere, the space between heart and thought,

Jim is.

And I will find him.

WHO TO WEAR

*"With loss, there is no ground, no certainty,
no reference point—there is, in a sense, no rest."*
—Pema Khandro Rinpoche

11.19

On the morning of Jim's memorial, C. calls. "There's a rainbow over the school that Jim designed," she tells me. She also says that she and H. saw an owl sitting in a tree, its breast lit by the sun. Then it spread its wings and flew through the rainbow. In Native American tradition, she notes, owls are messengers of death. I hear this and wonder: a rainbow and an owl seventy miles away, where we're having the gathering. *Jim, setting the stage? Really? A rainbow in icy, gray New Hampshire in November?*

As I get dressed for the service, I note that I'm sort of caring how I look, and feel ashamed, as if it is disloyal to Jim to have any trace of vanity. I've lost weight. The navy silk skirt fits me well. And K. has arrived with the gift of a deep, vibrantly blue sweater, as if she knows that there will be a flicker of my former self, wearing such a color.

My real Self is off wandering, seeking Jim, so at the memorial I find it hard to encounter people struggling with their own feelings about how I must be doing, what death is about, how we'll all go forward without him. The children are there and they love me and they love Jim and I can't reach through my wall of glass to reach them. I'm stuck in consideration of which mask to wear. The noble sufferer. The one who endures. The compassionate seeker. The shell-shocked husk. The whining child. The devout saint.

If there weren't the problem of this fog all around me, I'd know how to be. Or I'd just be. Without contriving a self.

I'd had visions of a stronger Rondi, like my immigrant Dutch farmer ancestors, who endured so many hardships and persevered so powerfully in their lives. But my head feels so swollen, it's hard to think. And the fact that I'm outside my body, watching me move my lips, hearing me talk without understanding what's coming out . . . I can't seem to manage. But I do wonder what this version of me looks like, and I am torn between thinking I should be taking care of people, feeling resentful that I need even move my body at all, and fearing that if anyone is kind to me, I will break apart into tiny, irretrievable pieces.

FINDING THE THREAD

*Not of the life of one, but of the life
of two who became one.*

Each stage of mourning takes me farther away from Jim. Yet, I said to him, in the weeks before he died, "We'll still be married, it will just be different."

I think I was trying to say, "We'll stay connected, I promise."

And I was trying to say, "There's a truth in why we found each other, and I'm not going to lose sight of that gift."

I was trying to say, "I don't know where you're going, but I promise you won't go there without my thoughts, without my love. Don't worry. You will never be alone."

How then, does that make sense here, alone in my home after the service, where the future stretches out before me like a vast empty corridor? Now, there is the shape of my life and what to do with it. Which piece of my Self must I take up alone, and which piece belongs to the question of how to be in relationship with what my heart says is still alive and true?

I go upstairs to our tiny bedroom with its big window looking down on the Green River and clear off one of the long shelves that is built into the wall at the foot of the bed. I put the pottery jar containing Jim's ashes on one side of the shelf and then I take the framed picture of Jim that sat on his coffin and put it in the middle. It's a black and white photo of him taken just before we married on a sunny day at an opening ceremony for the construction of the new Waldorf elementary school he designed. His hair is lit up and he's smiling, looking to his left a bit, and holding a large, twelve-sided geometric form made out of forged steel. This metal time capsule, with the written thoughts and dreams of faculty members inside it, is about to be buried in a corner of the foundation.

I sit down in front of his picture and just look.

And then, I suddenly realize that I'm seeing the real Jim.

It's the same "across a crowded room" vision that I had when we first met in England. That shock of recognition that this person is unique to you, not just in terms of what he does, but who he *is*, as if he has just touched down on the planet and you are lucky enough to be the only one who knows he is here— and he's looking at you with that same sense of awe.

I'm now realizing there's a vitality in that first vision that got submerged in the day-to-day challenges of building a life together.

The life review, the one that people report during incidents of drowning or other near-death experiences, passes through me. Only it's a review not of the life of one, but of the life of two who became one. Like a ribbony trail of vivid snapshots, I've arrived at our origins, that first moment of resonance.

I wonder now if I can cry—tears are buried deep and have been for days. But I'm caught up in gazing at Jim, feeling the stretch of awareness, like a visit back to the home that you grew up in and the places you found—a room, the crook of a tree, a meadow in early evening—where your solitude was your chapel.

Then, there is a ripple over the picture and Jim's face transforms.

For only the briefest of moments, it is brilliant with light. He looks ecstatic.

I gasp and burst into tears of surprise, relief, joy, wonder, confusion, loss. As if I've seen behind some curtain: *Is this where Jim is? Is this what he is experiencing?*

I feel left out, like a child not old enough to go to a party.

A GLIMMER OF TRUTH

You live with and love another person until you no longer need words to communicate. Why would you not also be able to feel this communion beyond death?

One day, then another, and another, passes by as I struggle to get my bearings. I don't know how to grieve. *Is this what it's supposed to be, this strange mixture of devastation and wonder?* Jim's out there somewhere, but somehow it also feels as though he's inside me. I feel, rather than hear, his voice resounding inside of me like a note of certainty and it's all mixed up with a protesting child who won't listen, who wants to have a tantrum instead.

Then, on the third evening, sitting in front of the small altar I've created, I tell him this. I close my eyes and try to find him. After a few moments, I see his face and he's looking at me very seriously, as if he's calling me to myself. And in that moment, I let go of self-absorption, fears, and grief and want to make him feel I'm okay. I want to tell him over and over that I will keep him in my heart while he goes through whatever he is experiencing now.

This is important, a glimmer of truth about grief.

I realize that part of it is about *poor me*, the harboring of a sense of deep injustice about my uprooted life path. The hard work ahead. But this has nothing to do with Jim—as if I could blame him or go to him, the gods, or Fate for sympathy. It's my own tangle to straighten out, and if I can face this truth I'll begin to accept that there is no way forward other than towards some greater awareness about the two of us. Then, ultimately, a fuller realization of the meaning and purpose of my life.

Dr. L. has reminded me that Rudolf Steiner said our remembrances, thoughts, and prayers are nourishment for the dead. But my heart is all closed up so that it won't hurt.

I realize that it can't love unless I will it to wake from its frozen state.

So, I try.

I focus my mind, look at Jim's face and shining hair and also focus on my heart, feeling its fragility, the tight squeeze in my chest. Going deeper through the ache, I reach back to the truth about Jim, the good fortune of Jim, the mystery of Jim.

And suddenly can take a breath.

I fill my heart with love. And I send him love like I'm a superhero, beaming it like a light out of my center, visualizing it move on a bright path to him.

It's not about loss in this brief moment, but about gratitude.

I cannot hold the energy very long before it fades from a deep, whole Self-awareness into self-consciousness and reflection. In this moment, I know: Love cannot function as an idea—a thought, a prayer—it must be a vibrant, whole-body experience, alive and wondrous—*but not accessible without purposeful engagement.* Not a negotiation, but something pure and uncompromised. I'm not sure I ever really understood this truth, other than organically, with my children when they were very young.

I'm realizing now that I can do this practice every evening, as well as at any moment when I feel lost. I can acknowledge the crossroads, where I will probably find myself, over and over, caught between a floundering self-pity and a promised commitment to selflessness. How can I transform without practice?

There's my purpose in the days ahead. I decide to commit to doing this nightly ritual for a year. Or longer. Who knows how it will change me? Certainly, I should feel no longer helpless.

Growing consciously through my grief will be about the choice. I'll have to choose to practice love, live that love is eternal.

I'm more centered now, but my voice still croaks as I decide to ask for help. I ask aloud, to hear myself, so I will pay attention. I'm asking Jim to help me, but not just Jim, because I have finally acknowledged that I cannot do anything alone. I just haven't figured "Who" is out there, but at least I commit to the connection.

Then, I'm inspired to give thanks, despite wondering, as I have been for months, who can hear me: *Infinite Spirit, Unnameable Word, God-by-my-own-definition, angels, Jim* ...

And yes, despite that other voice in my head that whispers that such petitions are futile gestures.

I've found a small ledge to stand on and with humility, I give thanks for the lessons that I hope to learn, for finding the thread that will guide me out of this labyrinth.

I do so, realizing that I am practicing acceptance of all that has been, and all that will be.

Stronger, calmer, I give thanks, and then crawl into bed.

CELESTIAL VITAMINS

*There was a vague, shadowy figure just outside of the
bedroom door. Rondi got out of bed quickly—
was it Jim? By the time she got to the door,
the figure was gone.*

11.24

I've been falling into deep sleep right after my new, before-bed
practice. I keep my evenings free of too much stimulation and
sit at my small altar, giving myself time to unload the self-
involved debris of the day, to complain, to voice my fears, to
cry, to shed. When I'm finished, I take my two hands and pass
them lightly, about an inch or so above my body, from above the
top of my head down to my feet. I learned this energy-clearing
practice from my older sister when she came to visit Jim and it
makes me feel calm, even take a few deep breaths.

I say aloud, "That was about me, now this is about you, Jim."
Then, I visualize Jim, focus on my heart, and send him love. I
ask for help and give thanks, returning before bed each evening
to the same practice of openness and acceptance.

As a result of this ritual, I've been sleeping as if I'm carried
off somewhere in the middle of the night and put in a fire and

cleansed. In the morning, I wake feeling peaceful and new, just for a moment. And then a curtain descends and Life steps forward to claim me—but not before I write down any dreams that I have before waking.

Despite the nights of deep sleep, when Life steps forth to claim me, it's clear that my body is full of unresolved stuff that I can't begin to identify. It is suggesting that grief could possibly even cripple or kill me. Or will it break my heart, even while I am trying to grow into a new state of being?

Both shoulders have contracted due to an excruciating case of bursitis. I can't lift my arms without whimpering in pain from the inflammation. Maybe I'm really just trying to disappear, pulling myself into a tighter and tighter ball of non-self. Except that my body is in the way, a taut frame of resistance that's cracking at the points of greatest strain.

When I get out of bed in the morning, sharp pain shoots through my feet when I stand. Perhaps they are contracting tightly while I sleep. They too, are suggesting my Self is attempting to abandon ship. I think maybe I'm trying to get out through the top of my head, like the Buddhists say the spirit does at death. I try stamping my feet and circling my bedroom, muttering, "I accept my life. I am willing to go on," and this comes out sounding shaky and tight.

My body is clearly struggling with the effects of acute stress. I've begun using *Ignatia amara*, a homeopathic remedy for grief. It takes the edge of vulnerability off when I venture out into public. Otherwise, I'm not one for pills, especially after witnessing how well Jim's whole being responded when he was no longer using conventional medicine.

I thought of adding meditation to my self-care, having practiced before, but after a few tries I find I'm too anxious and can't sit still, other than in my evening ritual. I'm hurting in places I did not know my body contained.

As I try to figure out how to manage all of the dimensions of grief, I'm doing some reading. Someone has given me *The Tibetan Book of Living and Dying*, a big, thick book on Buddhism that I cannot possibly digest. I skim through the pages about the process Jim supposedly went through as he was dying. *What good does it do me to know this?* I wonder. I can't relate to any of it now—when I need simplicity. Clearly these words come from a tradition that is enormously complex.

I have no family story that tutored me in what happens to people as they die; still, my tidy northern European ancestry is more familiar with stories of blinding light and comforting presences than with Buddhist descriptions of the "red essence of the mother meeting with the white essence of the father in the heart while consciousness dissolves."

I stop, however, with my dismissive critique when I read Sogyal Rinpoche's four-step prescription for how to grieve.

1. Invoke in the sky in front of you the presence of whichever enlightened being inspires you the most.

2. *Open your heart and call to him or her with all of the pain and suffering you feel. If you feel like crying, don't hold back; let your tears flow, and really ask for help.*

3. *Imagine and know now that the buddha you are crying out to responds, with all his or her love, compassion, wisdom, and power. Imagine that light as nectar, filling your heart completely, and transforming all your suffering into bliss.*

4. *As you do this practice again and again, saying the mantra and filling your heart with bliss, slowly your suffering will dissolve in the confident peace of the nature of your mind. Imagine you are sending this blessing to your loved one who has died. Through this practice you can feel consoled, encouraged, and empowered to help the dead person.*

As I read these words, I realize that I'm doing a version of this in my bedtime ritual. Number one on the list . . . the help of some enlightened being? Rinpoche says in his first sentence that I get to choose. Spiritual freedom. Trust yourself and whatever opens your heart—this I can say *yes* to. I still find myself suddenly able to take a deep breath whenever I inwardly ask the question: *Will I be okay?* That brief opening, however, is not sustained. Grief is work, it's said. For me, right now, I'm remembering Mammy's prescription for those hard times together with Jim: "Just keep moving." It means finding what will soothe me, comfort me, inspire me, hold me together from the inside all the way to my outer edges.

Despite knowing, deep down, that I am searching for a spiritual foundation, I remain a believer without a country. I don't want a god that is a thing or a name, a fixed definition. I want God as an experience that ignites every cell in my body to take away my pain. I'm coming to realize there is a path to such a realization, but I've only taken a few first steps.

I try Sogyal Rinpoche's advice a few times, call out for some enlightened being to find me when I'm overwhelmed with tears, but I struggle with apathy.

I have a friend who wants to bring me to a bereavement group run by the local hospice. I resist this too. My sense is that I don't want to process or analyze my newborn, evolving experiences through sharing—nor do I feel it will help me to become emotionally entangled in other people's pain. No help from my family either—we have no structure for dealing with death and anyway, Mom is still stuck in her own unresolved pain-world after losing Dad seven years ago.

My two children: We are loving and caring about one another from a distance. They are grown and busy working on their own lives, yet I know they mourn Jim and don't know quite how to deal with me. I'm sad that I haven't the strength to share more with them, but trust our relationship will work that part out when I'm stronger.

Bottom line: I guess I'm too resistant and incapable of taking any route but my own, yet I know that I could use someone to give me a sense of direction.

I finally decide to make an appointment to see Quang, the Vietnamese doctor who worked with Jim early on in his illness. Until the day when he'd folded his hands and told us so kindly that it was time to let go.

What I remember now, though, was the first thing that he had said to Jim, that the best way to deal with his illness, in addition to taking his herbal medicine, was to "remember your religion, every moment of the day and night." Quang made a gesture when he said this, indicating a point between his brows, that knowledge of religion was to be kept there.

Front and center, an unwavering beacon of light at all times.

What *was* Jim's religion and source of strength in the worst of times? He was a deep seeker, that I knew, but also deeply private. We never discussed this question.

A SMALL GREEN STONE

*"Like all explorers, we are drawn to discover
what's out there without knowing yet
if we have the courage to face it."*
−Pema Chödrön

11.30

Quang smiles kindly as I sit down at his small table and stretch out my arm for him to read the pulses in my wrist. His warmth provokes tears, so they slide down my face as he checks both right and left, eighteen pulses in all, according to his ancient Vietnamese medical training. He's like the computer the auto mechanic plugs into your car to get a readout on all of the systems. His three fingers rest lightly, then a little more deeply, then a bit more as he records the relative weakness or strength of the different bodily engines: lungs, heart, liver, spleen, small and large intestines, kidneys. Then he makes tiny, chicken-scratch notations in his book before sitting back and speaking to me.

"You have to just relax and let Jim go now," he tells me in his soft voice. "You have a lot of his sickness in your body and you need to clear it out. I will give you medicine for that. And

Jim needs to get used to being where he is, and you can help him by not calling for him to make things like they used to be. In a few months he will come back to you and see you."

Quang tells me how he went out into the streets and acted happy after his beloved father died, so that his father's spirit would not be held back by grief. "Now, my father comes and sees me often. I don't look at him though, but I know he is there. We talk. I ask him for advice. He takes care of me."

I listen to Quang because everything about him rings true. He was an abandoned infant adopted by a renowned Vietnamese healer, and survived the horrors of the Vietnam War to immigrate here to our tiny corner of New England. He is a master of martial arts and has practiced sorcery and studied ancient healing arts since the age of nine. When he was an adolescent, he spent five years studying with a master teacher in a cave seven miles deep in the heart of the "Touch the Sky at Noon" Mountains on the Cambodia–Thailand border. A life of spiritual discipline and endurance now manifest patience, kindness, and the gentlest of smiles on Quang's face.

In Quang's medicine room, where he prepares his medicines, there is a small altar on a high shelf where there are always flowers and sometimes an orange or two. I catch a brief glimpse of this heavenward ledge as he goes through the door— his gods look down on him as he begins to prepare herbal formulas for me to boil down into a strong, awful-tasting brew. I hear the sounds of mortar and pestle turning herbs to powder, the clang of a small brass gong as he prays over my medicine while he prepares it, and the rustle of paper as he makes neat packages for a weekly regimen.

He comes back into the treatment room and gives me six packets of dried leaves, roots, and flowers with a gentle warning not to touch the herbs with my fingers, because his power has been put into them and handling would dissipate the energy. I'm going to drink his prayers, a filament of strength all mixed in with the bitterest of tastes. It will discipline my body to shape up with such a concoction, I think.

It's been two weeks. As I negotiate the icy road back over the mountain pass that separates western Vermont and Quang from my home in the East, I ponder our talk about Quang's father and about the possibility of having contact with Jim in the future. It must be okay to send Jim love before bed each night because I'm practicing acceptance, rather than clinging to the past or denying the reality of my loss. All the same, I have to ask myself whether I have not wholly let Jim go if part of me is journeying across the universe to find him again.

I feel, however, that I'm not stuck on an agenda—I'm beginning to discern how much I can learn if I stay open. What I am holding, I believe, in my evening rituals, is an open space in my heart, where Jim can find a place, where I can grow a new heartful way of being.

I also think about Quang's words: I have Jim's sickness in my body. *Does Quang think I have cancer?* I can't begin to deal with that possibility. *He can't mean that.* I decide that he's talking about the energy body that Jim and I shared. *How could it not know cancer well? How could it not be lost and spent without Jim there to help me keep it whole?* I must have a cancer template on me. *I must be carrying that shrinking, hardening, devouring life-creeping horror in every one of my cells.*

I push such thoughts away with a shudder and leave it to Quang to help me heal. I'll deal with the work of restructuring everything else. The dread of illness is there, but it's not as great now as the challenge of living.

And yet, so much has already happened to the person I was. Facing death, holding it in my arms, changed me. A small voice tentatively suggests some of that newborn self is okay. It's only a small voice, because there's guilt attached to it, a sense that it's unfair to Jim for me to be surviving. But I can feel my shoulders beginning to loosen, even though my feet still contract at night while I sleep. Part of me is coming down into my body again; part of me is still trying to escape. I'm always cold though. All I want to do is sit by the woodstove and bake. I drink chamomile tea. I drink Quang tea. Jim's tee-shirt is my new camisole.

Back home, there's an icy wind around the house and the air smells of snow. I put an extra log in the woodstove, get close and open the mail. There's a card from L., whose husband died of cancer three years earlier. "Rondi, take it from me," she writes, "They say that when you are widowed, there are three things that you must do. The first is to go away for a while.

"And if you do this, the other two won't matter."

I have only a few savings, no job, no clarity about the future other than to know that it would be too painful to go back to the world of education, which I have been in ever since I married my first husband at age eighteen. And now I'm forty-eight. That Rondi is gone and I don't know what the new one wants. My sister has invited me to come to her home in England for the holidays. Yes, I will return to England, where Jim and I first met. My son and daughter will go too.

I decide I'll go afterwards to Iona. Jim spoke of his love for that tiny, rocky island off the coast of Scotland, when we first met in front of his watercolor of waves breaking on its shores. It is reputed to be the place where, around 563 CE the Irish abbot and missionary-evangelist Saint Columba first stepped on one of its white, sandy beaches. There, with twelve devoted companions, he founded an abbey as a base for spreading Celtic Christianity throughout northern Scotland. The resulting monastic community soon became a seat of learning and a place of pilgrimage. *So many prayers from across the centuries must be embedded there,* I think, *creating an island vibrant with revelations and hope.*

In the evening before bed, I add to my altar a small, jade green stone that Jim brought back from his time there. It's about the size of a large, slightly flattened olive and has a delicate, clearly traced white ring on one side. I reflect then that it is strange how the keepsakes of a loved one tell a history that you can never penetrate, but which holds something sacred and true about that person. This stone represents a part of Jim that I have always held in awe–a private, searching self that I could not access, whose thoughts and yearnings always seemed so much wider and deeper than my own.

Before bed, I am starting to say aloud a verse by Rudolf Steiner. It is becoming more rooted and strengthening as I commit it to memory.

> *Quiet I bear within me,*
> *I bear within my soul*
> *Forces to make me strong.*
> *Now I am filled with their glowing warmth.*
> *Now will I fill myself with my own will's resolve,*
> *And I will feel the quiet pouring through all my being,*
> *When by my steadfast striving, I become strong*
> *To find within myself the source of strength,*
> *The strength of inner quiet.*

As I "feel the quiet pouring through all my being," I find myself yawning and sighing and tension leaving my body. Thus, my nightly ritual takes shape, becoming my wise keeper with its prayers, pleas, and intentions.

Before blowing out the candle, I stroke the smooth surface of the green stone with my finger and think about how it traveled around with Jim, how he probably put his hand in his pocket at odd moments and rubbed it with his thumb.

I decide it's more of a seed than a stone.

I close my eyes and look for Jim and it seems he is sitting in his brown robe on a big rock near the sea.

ALL TANGLED BEAUTY
& DESPAIR

Rondi gets up on the little girl's horse with her, but she is quite unprepared for the ride.

The horse is blindingly beautiful. And the child is in complete control.

Rondi is without shoes and can barely stay in the saddle. Her perch is so precarious, she thinks to get down, but resists.

Her feet will sink into the muck below.

The child lets her down anyway, and goes off to jump her horse on her own.

Now, Rondi is back in her house when a serious, gray-faced man appears in the room. He heads out the back door, towards the place where the child is riding.

The child and horse have been injured!! "Why didn't anyone tell me!!?" Rondi cries, and runs over to them. The child is lying under the horse, beautiful, shining, accepting.

"Are you alright?" Rondi sobs.

The child says her legs won't work. But then she gets up and is okay.

The horse is fatally injured in the legs and groin and must be put down.

And the child won't accept this.

She vows to return home and nurse him to health again.

Rondi vows to help.

CHOOSING STARS & A TRIBE

*I'm on a time train, standing in the last car and pulling away
from Jim, watching him get smaller and smaller in the distance
as the days, like stations in a gray landscape,
unceasingly flash and fade along the track.*

12.13

One month. And one day. Moon waning.

What does it mean to lose the life I was in? Shock
disconnects. Our worlds seem to be so much a construction of
the mind, a collection of names and stories, a complicity with
others. But shocked beyond the known world, my perceptions
of time and space have lost their structure.

I've decided to acquire a yearlong calendar that records the
phases of the moon and the planets. *Is there a pattern to Jim's
travels through the heavens and my search for him in my
dreams? Might he appear when the moon is full, or in deepest
dark? Could Mercury, planetary symbol of communication,
cycle near and bring a message from him?*

I can envision that the planets cycle through both Jim's
limitless cosmos and my own. If I can find a pattern, then
perhaps I will find some peace, because a pattern revealed

between my inner life and the whirling lights in the sky will show me my loss was already recorded on a much larger scale than I might have imagined.

I say this because my father left on the same stars he rode in on, December 27, seventy-eight years apart and along with Halley's Comet too. Was it ordained? Significant? To our family, it made sense—Dad traveled on a singular path through his life, even while leaving trails of inspiration behind.

I only whisper this thought to myself because I feel the presence of the Scientist, that dismissive voice in my head reciting lessons about the psychology of the bereaved, labeling my experiences, like the rainbow on the morning of Jim's service, a "typical synchronicity," the shift in Jim's picture "anomalous, commonly reported in those with an imaginative cast of mind," the strong dreams and sense of two selves "dissociation, compensation for trauma, identity loss."

Such diagnostic labels tell me to seek no further or else risk losing my membership in consensus reality. Yet as the days go by, I am increasingly trading consensus for personal revelation. If I'm willing to travel in this unknown territory, my *yes* must be a key to open more doors.

I've acquired a copy of *A Grief Observed,* C.S. Lewis's record of loss after the death of his wife. He's like the participant-observer anthropologist who travels deep into a jungle to immerse himself in the culture of a tribal people, while nightly transforming back into his scientist self, and recording his studies in a journal. Lewis's book reads like a very British document, a reserved sort of grieving, several paces removed from howling about loss (which is not to say that he does not howl in private). But I relate to it because I, like Lewis, am in those same two bodies, one watching and recording, while the other flounders in deep waters, at times forgetting how to keep myself afloat.

Otherwise, yes, I've read about Kübler-Ross and the psychological stages of terminal illness, now also commonly applied to psychological stages of the grieving process. The stages to acceptance lead to through shifting attitudes of grief, fear, denial, anger, and hopeful bargaining for time and miracles, or perhaps in the case of the bereaved, bargaining for time to stop. But how does tracking such stages have anything to do with helping me keep my heart open? It feels like loss, with such a framework, is akin to having a serious, but predictable illness. It does not consider my small hope that loss can lead into a spiritual territory of mystery and personal growth.

I'm thinking about the term *conscious grieving.* As a child of the Sixties, I recall the introduction of the term *conscious childbirth,* for example, implying that the momentous experience of giving birth was a spiritual process, where preparation led to maintaining awareness throughout the birthing, rather than choosing drugs and/or surgery in order to not be present. It's also true that the goal of the anthroposophical protocol we employed during Jim's dying was designed to enable him to remain centered and strengthened spiritually, to practice *conscious dying*.

Did I accept the loss of Jim when he died, even while I sensed we were in the presence of great spiritual forces? It is too early to consider such a question. What I have now, however, is the nightly commitment to consciously practice love, gratitude, and acceptance. It is my soul space, my anchor, even while I otherwise struggle to find inner stability and islands of calm in each day.

.

ANTICIPATION &
REVELATIONS

*"There is a lantern in the soul which makes
your solitude luminous."*
–John O'Donohue

I feel less frozen now that I've made the decision to travel to England in a week. I've had a call from a friend, who, having heard of my desire to travel to Iona, tells me there is a retreat center there. She gives me a phone number.

I nervously dial the number in faraway Scotland. A man answers. Hearing a warm voice, I haltingly share my request and tell him about Jim. "My wife died a year ago," he tells me, and lets me know I will be welcome and that he will meet me at the ferry.

The thought that there is a surprising connection to my life waiting in Iona, a man who already has been tutored in loss and has surely found answers, creates a thrum of anxious anticipation in me. Partly because he's a man, I have to admit. The thought of an intimate sharing with him about the loss of our loved ones makes me feel deeply vulnerable. I'm not going to Iona to forget the loss of Jim, but to find him: *Will this man's presence help or hinder?*

In preparation for my trip, I dive into a frenzy of clearing, inside and outside of the house. I'm like the pregnant woman who madly cleans her home—nest building—when her body tells her she's about to give birth. There are tangles of branches from November winds all over the yard and a large, semifrozen mound of broken shingles from the roof job that Jim did last summer. The garage is full of junk—cardboard, papers, bottles, broken furniture, and tools. The branches go in a big burn pile for next spring. Everything else goes in our truck. I make trip after trip to the dump. Then I sell the truck too.

Underneath all of the mess, simple things begin to emerge: a polished wooden table against the window and the gray, empty river tossing beyond the glass. A neat stack of firewood on the porch. The red glow of the Oriental rug by the couch when the sun comes in in the morning.

Through all of this clearing, I know that I am circling around Jim's things, getting closer to touching them and deciding what to keep, what to let go. The fear of more pain has kept me at a distance, but the more I order the rest of my environment, the more at peace I become with approaching, at last, the part that holds the physical remnants of Jim.

I know that, in some way, I will be changed by taking myself away from this house and across the ocean. The pattern will be broken and something new will be required when I return. It will be January, a month of beginnings. Jim's death will be something that happened "last year," even though it will only be two months in the past. I decide to put treasured items in one old pine chest, so that however far away from home I might travel, I will be able to imagine them there, like a small fire kept burning on the hearth.

On Jim's desk, there is an old pair of cheap glasses that he got through England's universal health plan—funky, scratched, and somehow so intimate I cannot throw them away. They go in the chest with our love letters, our wedding rings made of woven wheat grass, and Jim's two treasured old tee-shirts from high school days, so worn they are almost transparent. They are like living beings, permeated with his scent, a unique, spicy sweetness that I could track blindfolded through a crowded football stadium, because every cell in my body has taken it in for nourishment. Before I put them in the chest, I bury my face in them and inhale like I'm taking an illicit drug, hoping for a rush of Jim to course through my veins.

And then I take the old gray one out of the box again and put it under my pillow.

Before my ten years' worth of writings go in, I open a journal from the time when we first fell in love, and read my description of Jim proposing. This is the first time in ten years that I've taken a look. When I come to the part about Jim asking me to marry him, I'm astonished to see that my handwriting suddenly transforms, becoming like his for several pages. I think of Jim's joke: *One of us is not necessary here.* Is this how destiny reveals itself?

Then I pick up and open his old, beat-up black leather address book. There's a force field of intimacy about it that makes me feel like an intruder. Since we did not marry until we were both thirty-eight, an entire history is recorded there from before we met.

Here was a bit of a sore place between us: I've always traveled light, shedding possessions and friends in my eagerness for each new experience over the next hill, impatient with memories of earlier selves that did not measure up to my sense of a someday better, smarter, more attractive me.

By contrast, Jim sometimes reveled in his past with such deep nostalgia that I felt forever excluded from some of the most treasured parts of his life.

As I turn the stained and yellowed pages in the small book, each woman's name causes pangs of jealousy; each man's name, a sharp sense of old friends and experiences he had without me. Now, I hold those memories in trust. I decide to contact some of those whose names I recognize, and especially some of his oldest friends who do not yet know that he is gone.

Then, I come to a tattered scrap of paper, tucked into the center of the book. It is a page torn from the program of a Bach oratorio.

Ah, stay then, my dearest life,
flee not so soon from me.
Thy farewell and thy early parting
bring me the greatest sorrow.
Ah, yes, tarry yet a while!
Else will I be entirely engulfed by pain.
Ah, stay then, my dearest life,
Ah, flee not so soon from me.

I'm deeply shaken, and read the words over and over, trying to make sense of the discovery. It reads as though Jim believed for many years that he was going to die. Was this deep depression? Or premonition? Or both? Did he want to die?

Why didn't I know? Why didn't I know?

12.18

Jim and Rondi are told that he's going to die. She wants to be brave and not cry in front of him, so she goes and lies on the floor in the other room and begins to sob. Jim comes to her, touches her on the hip—Ah, dear Rondi. I'm here, his touch says. She sits up and they hold each other. He hugs her hard.

I wake in tears from my dream; it was like I was watching myself in a play. Jim was whole when I hugged him, but I did not see his face—only the top of his head and his shining hair.

I can still feel the place on my hip where he touched me.

How to keep moving and not hang on, not probe old wounds for the sake of at least belonging to some part of him still.

My friend Linda writes, "After losing Jeremy, I spent a thousand dollars on shoes to keep myself here."

IONA

*"More often than not, we think pain is a signal that
we must stop, rather than find its source.
Our souls do not like stagnation. "*
—Malidoma Patrice Somé

I'm sighing deeply ever since our plane left the ground, feeling the web that entangles me in fear and grief in Vermont begin to loosen. As we descend and the intense green of the English countryside begins to break through the gray clouds, I feel as though I'm coming home. I'm reconnecting with a self that I have not visited for fifteen years. So much happened to me here during that time when I first met Jim. It was a chosen initiation, a personal quest that had been postponed by marriage at eighteen, two children, my demanding teaching and administrative job, and then the decision to divorce my first husband.

Yes, there was a structure to my visit: I was on sabbatical at a college studying the work of Rudolf Steiner. But in truth, back then, while searching for the strength to say *no more* to my volatile relationship, I was trying to grow up and find my reason for being. I was searching for the answer to one question: *Do I deserve to be here, in this life, on this planet?*

I sought the answer by skipping lectures and testing my fate bicycling and hitchhiking around southern England alone.

When I staggered against the wind on the edge of cliffs in stormy November and slept in an empty youth hostel under twelve blankets while the rain beat against the windows, I thrilled at the thought that no one knew where I was. If I survived, then I was meant to survive. My life would then have a purpose that was mine to discover.

Returning now to England is to reconnect with that adventurous, questing self.

12.30

My two children, Kyra and Marcus, have joined me. We meet at my sister's home in the English countryside north of London. It's a safe space, with deep gratitude for family mixed in with the sense that I am going through the motions in a life that is no more.

It is a relief to journey north to Scotland in the days after, heading to my New Familiar, the space I am practicing with Jim. It begins like a pilgrimage, first by ferry from Oban on the mainland to the port of Craignure on the big island of Mull, and then, in a car for thirty-five miles, a narrow track across a treeless landscape to another ferry at Fionnphort, where ten minutes in good weather takes you across the narrow strait to Iona, a bump of land only three miles long by a mile wide.

Wild rain, chasing clouds, tentative rainbows, heavy, white-capped waves—it is a voyage to a land out of time. As the Iona ferry leaps and rocks its way towards the small dock, I can see a few people waiting on the shore, clustered together under black umbrellas. And apart from them, a tall figure in a long woolen cape with a hood. The rain comes down to blur my vision as I negotiate the slippery gangplank and step onto the island.

The hooded figure approaches and greets me. Nervous, I am taken aback for a moment when the face, half-revealed under the dark hood, momentarily seems to be that of my father, dead nearly ten years. *Isn't this journey about Jim?* Peter briefly introduces himself and then leads the way through the sheets of rain to the retreat center, and sets me down with a cup of tea.

And then falls apart.

It is the anniversary of his wife's death and pain is etched all over his face. *He must be in his fifties or sixties,* I decide. I listen to his story with resistance because I have only just begun to find my own way to emotional stability and my hold on my strength is tenuous. Compassion, sympathy, sharing—none of these are in a place in me that I can access. I struggle with guilt at my clumsiness and disappointment that he seems to have no wisdom or insight to share after a year in retreat in this beautiful sacred place.

Peter tells me that he has been unable to make connections here and has become painfully isolated—especially from the local population. As I hear his litany of sorrows and hurt, I finally blurt out with impatience, "Why do you give them that power over you?" This, I realize, is both rude and pretentious, as if I could possibly offer any helpful counsel.

My question stops him, however. Longing to be free of his needs, I beg to be excused. He loans me a long, heavy raincoat and a pair of Wellington boots. With relief, I head out into the simplicity of rain and wind. And the wind is warm, even though it is a stormy, soaking New Year's Eve.

As I walk through the town, I pass cheerfully ragged yellow roses tossing in a garden and then follow a muddy track west, past pastures fenced with barbed wire that sheep have decorated with little white clouds of their wool. These I gather as I go, pulling, twisting, and winding the greasy fleece into a tight little ball of yarn. I imagine creating a thread that I'm following over the hill to Jim as I head towards the west side of the island.

Over a rise, and there is the ocean, leaping and crashing on a long stretch of white sandy beach. The water is turquoise, rather than New England gray, and there are colorful stones— reds, purples, whites, black, greens and gray—strewn all along the shore. My pockets soon become weighted down with treasures, but I have yet to find one that has the power of Jim's green stone. I want a special treasure that links me, now and forever, heart and soul, with this sacred place.

I'm becoming drenched as I wander along the shore, in and out of coves with cliffs and caves, stopping from time to time, transfixed by the sight of the waves, lively and playful. I draw and write in the white sand, then waves swallow my messages and carry them out to sea.

As I reluctantly head back in the dimming late afternoon, I see Peter in the distance, striding towards me to tell me he was worried that something had happened to me. I should be grateful, but his concern drains away the delight, communion, and empowerment I've known out in the wild weather and I struggle with resentment, although I'm polite enough.

I escape to my small room with its white wooden paneling, tiny window looking out on the bay and a radiator warming soft towels, which I wrap around my shoulders, feeling chilled and tired. But as I begin to relax on my narrow bed, the door suddenly opens and Peter is there. He begs that I allow him to lie down next to me and that I hold him. If only he can feel a woman's arms around him, once again, he says.

His grief unnerves me. I don't know what to do with it—mine is too new as it is. I don't know where such permission could lead. I'm getting stronger every day, but I'm not that strong; nor do I want this visit to Iona to be about taking care of him. Such intensity would, I'm sure, obliterate the small steps towards inner peace that I am making.

I am keenly aware that there are no other guests currently visiting the retreat center. The few staff are long gone home. Peter and I are the only ones here in this silent, otherwise empty building.

I say no, not unkindly, but no. He then begs me to come into the library, which is just down the narrow hallway. Feeling safer with this choice, I agree and follow him into the dimly lit small room and stand awkwardly while he moves to sit in a small chair, picks up a nearby guitar, and begins to play some melancholy jazz chords.

What is the meaning of this strange episode with a lonely, grieving man? The synchronicity throws me off. He could be a long-lost uncle, resembling my late father as he does. My beloved, inspiring, and complicated father, at his core, a lifelong spiritual seeker, left my mother devastated and furious after he died of a stroke. *Is this visit about my father or about Jim?*

Peter begins to sing a bitter, yearning version of the Stephen Sondheim song "Send in the Clowns." It's poignant and deeply sad.

I feel utterly overwhelmed and inadequate, and stand awkwardly by the door, longing for the song to be over. I finally say something inane, bid Peter goodnight, and escape to my room. But now I don't feel safe there, so I put on warm clothes and slip out into the night, determined to stay away from the retreat center, maybe all night even, or at least until it feels safe to go back to my bed and be undisturbed.

Outside the rain has stopped, the weather is damp and cool, and in the tiny village the cluster of stone houses are silent and mostly dark. I wander aimlessly through the few cobblestone streets, feeling I'm going to endure some long and tedious hours. But then, I round a corner and come to a stone building that is blazing with light and festivity. I tentatively peer inside, discover it is the local community's New Year's celebration, a real Scottish *cèilidh,* and I am welcome to crash the party.

I can't believe my good fortune—no isolated and lonely evening, but an authentic celebration of friendship and family at the turn of the year. Inside, there are farmers, tradesmen, shopkeepers, teenagers, ruddy-cheeked children and infants, retreat house staff—who might be missing? No one it seems, except Peter. There are games, a raffle, recitations, and skits, bagpiping, a young boy fiddling up a blizzard of notes, and one dance after another.

Then, it's midnight. I am pulled in to join their circle and with hands crossed with our neighbors, we all belt out "Auld Lang Syne" as we contract in, in a sort of big, laughing, community hug, then expand the circle out, in and out, faster and faster, to conclude at last with a cheer.

Breathless and joyful, I bid everyone goodnight.

A million stars are out now, after the rain.

As I walk back to my room, I realize that it is the first time in more than a year that I have given myself permission to experience my playful, happy self. I seem to have agreed to rejoin the human family and trust there is much still to fill my heart. Yes, grief is a hard journey. And even laughter seems to be essential as well.

In the morning, Peter and I have an uncomfortable breakfast together and neither of us mentions the night before. To fill the space, I blurt out some self-revelation, sharing about Jim's mother and her tough ways that leave me obsessing that someday I will hear that she knows well all of the ways that I failed her son.

Peter gives me a parting shot that I deserve, perhaps the key "Know thyself" lesson for both of us to come out of this strange encounter: "Why would you give her that power over you?" Peter asks me.

It's a pale, sunny morning and after the short ferry ride back to Mull, I wait for a bus that will take me back to join my family in Craignure. I leave behind at the bus stop a rather large heap of beautiful stones that I finally accept I will not be able to lug back home. But there is a small collection that must come with me, including "my stone," the companion to Jim's. It is a little bigger than a half dollar, a gray, flattish disc with a white spiral swirling on the surface.

It looks a bit pregnant, which pleases me enormously.

THE DIFFERENCE BETWEEN

"We must first have experienced the Divine
in ourselves if we are to discover it in the world."
—Rudolf Steiner

1.5, evening

Emerson College, Forest Row, southern England

I've arrived at the study center for the work of Rudolf Steiner,
and the place where Jim and I first met. In the small attic room
where I'm staying during the college holiday, I've done my
evening practice and climbed into bed, falling now into
reflection about recent days.

Despite the strange encounter with Peter, something was
affirmed during the pilgrimage to Iona that leaves me more able
now to look outward towards making a new life—not without
the spiritual grounding that my practice gives me, but because
of it, I believe. I'm feeling calm and strong, and in a different
place with Jim tonight.

In the morning, I hike uphill to an enormous oak tree in a
field overlooking the college. It is a cold, sunny, windy day and
although it is January, many birds are heralding signs of spring.
I sit down in the same place where I sat thirteen years ago. The

same great branch stretches out towards the Ashdown Forest in the distance and the hayfield grasses are glistening in the sun and wind.

It feels peaceful here, under the oak—a welcome sensation because I had a good cry on the hike up, shedding my feelings of overwhelm at having nostalgia and longing crowd in. This ancient tree knows me already, which is why I chose it for shelter and companionship during a personal vigil I undertook during the year I spent here as a student. I was pushing then, as I am in a different way now, to find a core of strength and awareness in myself that would confirm my existence.

During that year, I decided to sit outside under this oak and study the change of light from six o'clock at night until six in the morning. It was early spring, a time when Mars, Saturn, and Jupiter were reported to be in a triangular conjunction in Libra, my birth sign—and although I did not really understand the import, I did know that in astrology, triangles were positive and square conjunctions were not. I imagined perhaps those three planets would bring good energy into my life.

During that twelve-hour period, there was some boredom, some fear of the darkness, some hunger, some dozing. And then, there was also a life-changing experiment that had an extraordinary outcome. On that resolutely cloudy night, it occurred to me to see if I could focus my mind, or some aspect of my consciousness, and clear the skies in order to reveal the predicted configuration of the three planets.

There was a sense of "allowing" and "intending" all at the same time--being present, focused, and open, but without the emotional weight of wishing and forcing anything to happen. Thus, perhaps because I was in a sort of trance state, half awake, half asleep, having sat so quietly over the hours since nightfall . . . the heavy sky cover began to thin and then gradually fade away above me.

Within perhaps ten or fifteen minutes of effortless presence . . . there it was . . . a triangle of three brilliant planets shining in a hole in the clouds! While all else remained heavy and overcast.

How long was the reveal? I don't remember--maybe five to ten minutes long? But only that one part of the sky cleared.

What I do remember now, is that it felt as though the power to connect in such a way with the heavens came not out of my mind, but out of my center, almost as if I opened that hole in the clouds with energy from my core.

As I sit under the oak now, reflecting on the mystery of that long-ago celestial response to my attempt at manifestation, I become very calm and open. I think of the passage in T.S. Eliot's poem "East Coker," about the power of contradictions--about waiting without hope, love, faith or even thought--and thus we find a place where nothing can at the same time contain everything, and stillness "the dancing."

It seems to me now that spiritual awareness is built out of a practice of embracing contradictions.

Just as my time on Iona turned out not to be about mourning, but the beginning of healing, I realize that my visit here at Emerson does not have to be about nostalgia and grief, even though those can still grip me powerfully, often without warning.

I am beginning now, with a little trust, to consider more deeply my present and my future.

I spend the next few days in the college library, reading about life after death, including revisiting Elizabeth Kübler-Ross's work and that of near-death researcher Raymond Moody. His explorations of mirror-gazing, originally used by ancient Greeks to contact the departed, intrigue me. The practice involved creating an altered state of consciousness, during which the participant would sometimes see apparitions of a departed loved one. Would such approaches one day become a normal part of grief work in the future? I think perhaps we bereaved have a hard time finding peace without contact from our loved ones "just one more time." I observe this longing in myself, despite the dreams in which Jim already shows up from time to time.

It is Rudolf Steiner's writings though, that challenge me to simply accept my capacity to experience the truth of life after death. Again, I encounter his words about the importance of spending time reading to or thinking about the dead. A skeptic might call it self-hypnosis or some aberration of grief. Maybe someday I will know for sure what is right and possible for love to achieve across the boundary of the two worlds. I'm still doing my evening practice, but it's shifting in focus. Now Jim's physical presence seems more distant, but his spirit less so.

Steiner can be challenging to read, but I enter easily into the truth of these words by a student of Steiner's work named Roy Wilkinson:

> *We may see a plant, we may know all the substances within that plant, we are aware of the influence of Sun, earth, air, and water, but we do not perceive with our ordinary senses that force which makes the plant grow. Here we approach the borders of a supersensible world. If another consciousness could be developed, we should be aware of it.*
>
> *We see the physical world with the physical eye. To see the spiritual world, we need to develop a "spiritual" eye.*

It feels as though I've had a sense for what may be experienced in numerous ways "beyond the physical" for a long time. But I'm a lazy, chaotic seeker, have found it hard to stick with anything. Until now. It's taken a deep loss to reawaken the hunger to explore.

Wilkinson's words relate to another challenge I created for myself when I was here fifteen years ago. I had been at Emerson for six months, part of the time madly falling in love with three different men (Jim being one of them) and sobbing regularly from loneliness, high drama, and fear. The rest of the time I would sometimes play hooky from class, get on my bicycle and head out alone on adventures around southern England, never knowing where I would end up sleeping at night. I was collecting small triumphs, like learning that it's possible to sleep alone under the stars on top of an enormous grassy mound in Glastonbury (reputed to be one possible location of King Arthur's Camelot) and still survive.

When spring came, I decided to sequester myself in my room for thirty-six hours, blindfolded and fasting, while I explored my surroundings with my other senses. When I woke on the morning of that exploration, remembering to keep my eyes closed, my first act was to reach for the carpet next to my bed. The wool rug, which felt warm and prickly, was, surprisingly, a form of nourishment. Touch, rather than sight or food, would inform my day.

I rose and began to move around the edges of my small bedroom, identifying the contents of my life: my clothing, books, memorabilia. When I came to the windowsill, I felt my way along, touching and handling the collection of various objects that had come my way and were chosen to treasure. There was a vibrantly fresh daffodil. Some rough shells and smooth, sinuous pieces of wood.

Then, my fingers found two small, round objects of identical size. One I recognized as a chestnut and the other, a stone.

What has stayed with me is this: I could tell which was which by merely touching each lightly, with the tip of my finger. I had never realized that my sense of touch had such intelligence.

The nut, the seed for new life, without being held or weighed, felt hollow and light. It felt "awake."

The stone felt dense and hard. Not dead. Not even asleep. Eyes closed, I could sense it contained a profoundly condensed history of process and evolution.

This was a surprise: life potential versus life past.

Remembering this now, I'm reminded of my astonishment that I was able to feel invisible energies in Jim's body when I held his head to ease his pain.

I am caught now by these sentences from one of Steiner's lectures, "The Dead Are With Us":

Regardless of which religious belief we hold, or if any belief, all we need is our own body, for it alone is the instrument to directly witness the spiritual knowledge we hold deep within. If we only allow ourselves to go within, develop our inner life with practice, we can know and experience the great mysterious and spiritual depth of our being.

1.16

It's the last day of my visit. As I walk through the yard of Plaw Hatch Farm next to the college, I come to a pen full of half-grown calves. One calf has her beautiful head stuck under the fence, her budding horns preventing her from drawing back from under the metal rail. It's a challenging puzzle, to be sure. She had obviously worked her way forward for a taste of fresh grass and then found no easy way to go backwards.

I kneel down, wondering how I can find the strength to twist and turn and push her heavy head back, and whether I should go look for help. But the farmyard seems to be deserted at this time of day.

Something now inspires me to take the calf's head in my two hands and, with a kind of gentle, openhearted intention, such as I used to shift the position of Jim's head when he was in pain, I find I can easily turn the calf's head and with only a slight effort, release her. It seems as though she comes completely under my power when I touch her that way.

Or could I say that I gave in to letting "something else" do the work?

I walk on, feeling slightly mystified, yet triumphant, with that so simple, wordless communication.

Did I find Jim on Iona? Or here at Emerson College, where we first discovered something between us that would not be left alone? It's true, I have been visualizing Jim for months, sitting in his brown robe on a rock on the edge of the sea. But if I went to Iona to look for Jim, I think now it was not for Jim himself, but for something essential about Jim—whatever moved him so deeply when he was there. There was/is in him, something that has always left me with a sense of awe. *Is this how deepest love awakens, when it touches an essential knowing, a certain mystery, about the person you get to share your life with?*

There is something stirring in me that I hunger to know better and am beginning to trust that I am capable of learning.

I'm ready to go home.

THE SECOND QUESTION

SOUL

WHO AM I WITHOUT MY BELOVED?

CHOICES

"You have a right to be here. And whether or not it is clear to you, the universe is unfolding as it should."
—Max Ehrmann

1.25.94, 10:30 PM, Keene, New Hampshire

A snowstorm, a slippery bus ride, and my sister Andrea to meet me.

Home is blanketed in snow. The river is mute under slabs and humps of ice and drifts. Silence, silence. The exhilaration I found in being stretched and challenged by my trip subsides now as memories, loneliness, and our enormously empty small cottage forces the inevitable question: *What now?*

I'm in a new place in myself, to be sure. The question of my soul is really "Who am I without Jim?" I've been a wife, mother, teacher, and administrator since I was nineteen and, except for the period of rebellion and divorce when I was thirty-three, followed by remarriage to Jim at thirty-eight, I've never had my self alone to think about. But now, my children are beginning new lives far from home. The future is mine to define, compromised by a lack of savings and income, but I have enough to give me a little space to figure things out. One thing I know for certain: I don't want to go back to the life I had before.

Who am I without Jim in my life? How does a middle-aged woman (*ouch*) plan her future when everything she had believed she could trust is uprooted? I feel old, as if life has taken me past a point when I can begin a career. I find myself asking "What sorts of professions are still marketable until one's final breath?" Something in the arts, yes, because true artists, I believe, never stop growing and deepening their search for authenticity and self-expression. The healing professions, yes. The more venerable one becomes, the more credible.

Teaching, of course, which I've been around all of my adult life, but not with mastery beyond the fiber arts, which I taught myself while a faculty wife. Then, there is my history as a school admissions director and marketer—work that was creative for the times and circumstances in which I did it, but not for any future that I can envision for myself.

Devotion to personal growth characterizes my current choices—and there may be others that do not presently attract my interest.

What my pondering leads me to is the sense that I want to live the rest of my life with the kind of freedom that will allow me to continue to challenge myself to grow spiritually and creatively.

I am beginning to whisper to myself about a long-held dream of a career as a writer. At the same time, I wonder about becoming a grief counselor. Have I learned anything that might help others in a similar situation? These two visions may strengthen over time, that of an unmet longing for self-expression, the other of a life experience that could become a call to service.

These I can see, can help me find meaning, purpose, and direction. Both visions, however, are a big step for someone who has struggled with insecurity and shyness all of her life.

During my first year at Emerson College, I came across an anecdote told by famed art dealer Ambroise Vollard concerning the painter Paul Cézanne, whose career he helped shape. At a gathering, Vollard writes in his memoir, Cezanne was approached by a society woman who, gushing over his work, asked him to teach her how to paint.

Cézanne's reply: "Madame, if you wish to become an artist, force yourself to develop personality!"

At first read, a humorous putdown. But truly, I've always needed and loved this story. Find the courage to go your own way. Be willing to risk everything–loneliness, poverty, ridicule–in order to find your own truth.

Make your life a work of art, however you wish to define it.

Clarity. Be clear about what you do, think, say, and especially, ask for.

At last, I make a commitment. I will give myself three years to see if I can create a living as a writer. If I fail, I will choose another path then. But meanwhile, that block of time will help me develop plans and keep me clear about my choices. Will I write about losing Jim? *Not for a long time*, I think. I need to mature and gain perspective. I'm going to trust that the vision will find its own way to manifest when the time is right.

I'm a forty-eight-year-old woman who has only published a few letters to an editor in the local newspaper, plus created promotional material for schools. But I've loved to write since I was young. If there was a family fight, I could not wait to take pen to paper and recount the story, usually with humor. I've never forgotten the English teacher who put exclamation points all over the pages of the first essay I ever wrote.

I will have to find ways to support myself, meanwhile. Knowing how easily I become absorbed into any project that requires creative thinking, I resolve to only take simple jobs that do not divert my energy, but keep food on the table.

And meanwhile, what will get me thorough the dark, frozen days until spring?

I need warmth, sensuality, inspiration, a plan. I long to spend the winter in a greenhouse, with flowers, the smell of damp earth and scented, humid air. Having once taken courses at Smith College, only a forty-five-minute drive from my home, I search in their catalog and am excited to discover a horticulture class. I enroll just in time for the new semester.

I can feel myself suddenly eager to explore again, the way I felt before I traveled to Iona.

As ideas and hope crowd in, a small voice asks, *Will this decision lead my time and attention away from exploring my connection with Jim? Is this a good choice? Part of my process?*

I trust that keeping my heart open, asking for help, and accepting the lessons as I continue my nightly practice will keep me on the right path.

FROM NOUN TO VERB

"In truth, I doubt if anybody ever does really see a mountain, who goes for the set and sole purpose of seeing it. Nature will not let herself be seen in such cases. You must patiently bide her time, and by and by, at some unforeseen moment, she will quietly and suddenly unveil herself, and, for a brief space, let you look right into the heart of her mystery."
—Nathaniel Hawthorne

I'm a poor student at Smith College, unable to focus but thrilled to be able to inhale beauty and fecundity in the greenhouses, as I had hoped. The smells, warmth, moist air, and loveliness of flowers and damp earth lead me into thoughts of our garden at home by the river, designed in a mandala of circular beds around a central arch. Jim called it "The Dancing Woman," with a circular rose bed for her head, the archway her heart, a sweep of grass her skirt, and a well in the grass, her womb. I long for spring and the ability to get my hands in the soil again.

I can say that the first "book" I ever created was a thick journal of my notes and images of this garden—and this leads me, one day in the greenhouses, to remember an extraordinary moment there in late summer.

Our land along the Green River runs north to south, with a steep, heavily forested ridge across the water on one side and a dirt road and collection of meadow and wetland on the other. There is something about this configuration that makes the light transcendent as the sun lowers in the valley, with every leaf and petal illuminated.

One August afternoon, I stepped into the garden and suddenly experienced it as described by Nathaniel Hawthorne: "Nature will, at some unforeseen moment . . . quietly and suddenly unveil herself, and, for a brief space, let you look right into the heart of her mystery."

I wrote afterwards in my journal:

Here stood the many-branched sunflowers in banded maroon and gold, and there, the marigolds and purple cosmos spread by the blue-leaved cabbages and spilled into the path.

Lifting, then burying themselves to purr and drone in the flower centers were fat and avid bumblebees. Above and through them, monarch butterflies touched down at random—a medial whisper lost and found—here by the rugosa, there by the beebalm.

Transforming the uppermost layers of air were the goldfinches, breezing from sun-face to sun-face, pecking and twittering coloratura at the nourishing spirals of seed, scattering the bounty for winter-tunneling mice and future seasons.

I did not see, so much as feel, the colors, the movement, the song.

My garden in that single moment was transformed from a noun to a verb.

Memory will only shadow that brief, inner flash of knowing.

That particular experience of my autumn garden as a single, energetic, interweaving being reminds me of the brief moment I had with Jim's picture after his funeral, the transformation into a vision of something wordless, eternal, and ecstatic.

I begin to dream of creating a spiritual garden book. I have not thought before that our experiences with gardening were more than just loving the beauty of our artful piece of work. The garden was a noun, our glorious "thing." After that August afternoon, I realized how limited my awareness had been. I didn't want to garden alone anymore. I didn't want to think about the garden, I wanted to know it, to acknowledge and deepen my experience of Nature's own design at work.

I couldn't imagine then how to make the transition from defensive, albeit appreciative authority to responsive partnership, but I knew it meant altering my way of connecting.

Maybe it meant forging a relationship with the intelligence and beauty I had seen.

How might I share what I learned?

Ideas crowd in. I visit the Smith library, put on white gloves, and so very reverently turn the pages of medieval herbal manuscripts, marveling at the colorful paintings of healing plants, like pictures of small gods, filling entire pages with their grandeur and power.

When Quang makes his herbal medicine, he knows his herbs, bark, seeds, and fruits intimately, as living energies. His prayers intensify their power in me, demand my reverence for their divine gifting.

How capable are we modern gardeners of experiencing such authority in our own gardens?

The possibility of bringing something worthy into the world gives me a direction and a purpose. Something in me is coming alive again.

FORCE FIELDS

Faith is allowing yourself to be loved.

"Will you marry again?" a friend asks me. I have finally begun
to reach out to my community. They are less intimidated by my
grief, I think, and I am less afraid of their kindness breaking me
apart. But what about finding love again? I can't begin to
consider that possibility now. Something is growing within me
and with Jim—I don't want to lose the thread.

I was an awkward, shy, taller-even-than-my-third-grade-
teacher, dreamy kid. The kind of child who tries to become very
small and obsequious when dealing authority figures. I
mention this because one byproduct of surviving loss is that my
voice has lowered into a more grounded, calmer register. I no
longer squeak in a don't-hate-me, little girl voice when
conducting business with strangers over the phone. Because,
it seems, there's nothing to fear when the worst thing possible
has happened to you.

Tragedy as a mantle of protection? Not really good if it's
only about anger and bitterness. Okay if it's grounding in a
deeper sense of security about myself. I know death, I have held

it in my arms. There is power in this—who would have thought this could be true?

All the same, I do feel a deep vulnerability around men, as if they have a force field around them heightened by my loss. I have not imagined that I would wear a mantle of widowhood for the rest of my life, despite saying to Jim as he was dying, "We'll still be married, it will just be different." And I feel this, that our relationship will be eternal. But if my destiny includes another relationship, I will be open to it. A fixed idea for my future would deny the work I am doing to learn how to trust my life and reason for being here.

It's not about being a widow though. Or even in a relationship. Right now, it truly is about that other question: Who am I without this person in my life? I have been a mother and/or wife since I was barely an adult. How could I give up finding the answer in favor of submersion in another relationship?

There was a moment, a few years into our marriage, when I was engaged in some sort of project, and while my mind was focused on it, I thought to call for Jim in the other room to ask his opinion. But I didn't call his name, I called out, "Fred?" The name of my first husband.

I was embarrassed and surprised when this happened—because there was no doubt in my mind that Fred would never have been whom I wanted, either then, or ever. There was no love between us, even when we married, which sort of happened because, in some old-fashioned way, we thought that sleeping together had to take us there.

I could see that Jim, when he arrived, had heard, and was unnerved by my mistake, which made me feel deeply guilty and without an explanation for what had happened. We glossed over it. But I was left wondering if there was something in me— or in marriages, in general—that sometimes relates to a partner as a *generic inhabitant* of one's "need space." Am I alone in this?

In me, I recognize that I do love my own company a great deal for someone who would reconsider marriage. Which points to the necessity to truly be aware and focused on what it takes to balance a relationship with my inner drives and passions—a daily practice of keeping a heart space for these alone.

Now, I am questioning everything about myself in this regard. *Maybe I'm not made for relationships? I love my solitude, but to give up hugging and holding with a soulmate? Sex? Creative companionship? Friendship with someone who recognizes that you're a flawed work in progress and loves you anyway?*

While I'm considering these and other paths, a friend asks me, "Have you been angry yet?"

This confuses and annoys me. "Why would I be angry?" I counter. "Jim could not help getting cancer." *I'm practicing acceptance, not self-pity,* I tell myself.

And yet, the idea of why anger and what it might look like pushes at me.

CLOSET OF DREAMS

"Dreams are the guiding words of the Soul."
—Carl Jung

I've been filling my journal with dreams that occur almost every night. It seems that I have to train myself to remember these fragmentary visions about myself, or myself and Jim, or Jim alone. A friend told me that I must become aware during sleep—or when I am just on the edge of waking—that a dream is occurring. And then, before even moving a muscle, I must wake myself up enough to go over the details with my conscious mind.

Not moving is important, confirmed by my own experience. If I open my eyes or shift my position at all, most of the dream thins and evaporates in the light of consciousness. On days when I am able to capture and retain the flow, however, I reach for my journal and make notes before it dissipates. These captured impressions are creating patterns and providing me with a history of how I am figuring things out—and of any progress I am making in processing my loss.

Sometimes I'm fully in a dream and other times I'm watching a character named Rondi, as if I'm in a sort of trance state. But my Big Dream when I had a conversation with Jim was unlike any other—extraordinarily real, eternally memorable, and life changing.

At least I've evolved enough by now to recognize that my dreams seem to fall into general categories, which repeat often enough that I am beginning to interpret them mostly as conversations with my waking self, telling me what's happening on a deeper level.

Dream series A. Almost-but-not-quite Jim (dreams of Jim, where he feels real, but untouchable and uncommunicative, I call this My Search. But I could also imagine that he's "checking in." And that's nice to ponder).

Series B. Dwellings in various stages of disintegration or with limitless rooms and corridors (My past life and future, with lots of seeking and not much finding. Sometimes, a house can be my body though, I think. Or even my brain?).

Series C. Overwhelm. (I find myself in the middle of a crowd or a dance, unable to create order or to stop trying to please a multitude of people. A lesson about Pathologically Pleasing behavior by an uncentered, insecure me).

Series D. Transport. (Cars, trains, even skiing or sliding around barefoot. Inevitable time passing, no brakes, being out of control).

Series E. Ice and snow, frozen rivers (My walk through Death Country—which happens to be quite beautiful and compelling, actually).

Series F. A young girl. (This seems to be a version of me who is innocent, beautiful, and sort of a bystander when the grownup me is also present. She's much more capable of dealing, it seems. Her innocence seems to be a kind of power).

Series G. Reports from the Field (dreams of Jim reported by friends and family), such as:

From my dearest friend M.: *I went to bed around 11:30 and the cat was purring next to me on the other pillow. I was listening to the cat and the rain and drifting off, when suddenly I was startled by the distinct sound of a male voice calling, "Helloooooo . . ." It woke me fully and I looked around in the moonlight and saw no one. I went back to sleep and began to dream.*

There was a blankness in the dream and then I saw a face hovering above me, looking down on me. The skin of the face was hanging down the way it will when you are in this position. And I was on my back looking up.

I thought it was Jim and asked, "Are you Jim?"

He answered, "Yes." His face was not serious, simply there, and he was bald. His eyes were piercing, but not unkind.

From Mammy: *I went to bed grieving because Jim has not contacted me. And then, while my eyes were closed, I saw a vision of a hand resting on a piece of paper and holding a pencil. And it began to draw the outline of a telephone. When the outline was finished, my phone rang and woke me up. And I heard Jim laughing!*

In many dreams, Jim appears only in fragments, not the whole Jim. I will see him, but at times, only part of his face, above his nose, with his eyes looking at me so seriously. Or I have a sense of him standing just outside the door. It feels as though he is waiting for me to reach him without complications. Just simply, directly.

But how? In a few dreams, I feel his touch when I wake. Are these sensations truly Jim, or bodily impressions of my longing for him? Are they vibrations of that single psychic body that we created together? I'm thinking (it's just my own thought) that the psychic body that two lovers create between them is where most of the activity of dreams, messages, and visions occur, and that after one half of the body withdraws from life, whether by death or absence, the whole shared body gradually dissolves.

The resonance of a psychic body with Jim developed because of everything we shared: lovemaking, breath, our watery selves, our thoughts and feelings, touch and holding, even the pulse of blood and energy every time we lay together. Over time, communication between us was based not on shared information but on intuitive knowledge, love, and understanding.

All the same, my earthbound self longs for physical verification, for sight and sound. I can't help it. I long for a Big Dream, a forever memorable, vivid revelation that tells me all is well with him. A dream that allows me to tell him . . . something. Words will not come now. I send him love every night, but still I have to ask: *What is not fully realized in myself? Where am I blocked?*

What about Quang's advice to let Jim go, and that he'll come back to me someday? Have I done this yet? Am I giving freely, waiting without hope, just holding the space open?

Is the inner process of letting Jim go another version of allowing and intending, being both relaxed and focused? I have to accept that the waiting for Jim really does have to be for its own sake.

How do I access the part of me that seemingly was able, while I was spending a night under an oak tree in England, to clear a hole in a cloudy sky and witness a brilliant planetary conjunction?

Recently, I have been having recurring dreams that I am walking near a frozen river. The ice is thinning and cracking open in places, and there is clear, crystalline water underneath. It's mesmerizing, spell-binding, and I long to jump in.

There is even the sense that something wonderful will happen if I do, but there's not quite enough of an opening.

It's now February. The Green River still carries its usual lid of luminous ice and glittery drifts of snow. Yet the light comes sooner now in the mornings and it is beginning to seem as though something, somewhere, is melting. Because the water running under the ice has increased its force.

BREAKTHROUGH

"Where there is great love there are always miracles . . .
One might almost say that an apparition is
human vision corrected by divine love."
—Willa Cather

2.10
Dark of the moon and I felt sad and lonely all day. Returning from the Smith College library in my car, I began half-listening to a tape on Buddhist thought. And then, I heard the teacher say: *"The greatest gift anyone can give to another is their own death."*

I immediately thought of Jim dying so that I could grow spiritually. The thought was devastating. I kept seeing his face during a time the week before he died, his eyes full of tears, one tear constantly sliding down his left cheek, me reciting a prayer while gently wiping the tears away.

I cried a good part of the way home in the car, then muddled through dinner. At bedtime, tears turned into a full-blown tantrum and I ranted and raved for a long time. The deeper I got into my misery, the more bubbled up to the surface.

I poured out my grief and sense of inadequacy. I was furious with Jim. I hated my life. Shouting, sobbing, pacing in my small room. I was so sick of trying to be spiritual. I wanted Jim back in my life. To hell with acceptance, I felt abandoned. *Why didn't he fight harder for me, for us, to stay here?!*

Incensed and bitter, I reached for an angel card. Maybe I was hoping to get a message of love. *"Transformation."* I drew another and another: *"Surrender." "Simplicity." "Strength." "Peace." "Beauty."*

Blank. I would have laughed then, had I not been so distraught. It felt like getting the message, "Oh, fill in whatever you need, we're outta here!"

I put myself to bed spent, unloving, unthankful, and exhausted.

* * *

I'm going to see Jim. He is at a school on a hilltop, the one where I had worked and which he redesigned after he first moved to New Hampshire. I park at the bottom of the hill and ascend. The snow has receded, leaving an open track winding upwards. Spring is coming, and the track is muddy, with frozen earth underneath. At the top, I walk across a wide, flat, barren field.

I come to the main building at the end of the track. And there, at long last, I see the whole, entire, fully present Jim!

He is coming down the front steps, his arms piled high with loaves of fresh-baked bread in white paper sacks. He is laughing and crowing triumphantly over his wealth of food. He is no longer starving and wasting away!

He smiles widely at me when he sees me, but he's not surprised, it's as if seeing me is an everyday occurrence.

"Put down the bread and give me a hug!" I cry.

He puts down the bread. And holds out his arms.

I rush into his embrace and hug him hard and long. Right cheek to right cheek. Feeling the warmth of his skin, I'm bursting with joy and relief.

We sit down together on a nearby grassy mound bordered by a wall. He leans against it with one knee up, me sitting sideways with my hand on that ever-bony knee. He looks thin and pale, like one does after a long illness, but he's definitely on the mend. His eyes are clear and there is a flush of increasing vitality about him.

His still-bald head is covered by a light blue silk scarf, pirate-style. I can see around the edges of the scarf that his hair is growing back. And he is wearing his old red plaid shirt. He looks profoundly happy and excited, not about me specifically, but about his present circumstances.

Not about me, because he's not surprised to see me. Because I'm nothing new, just his wife paying him a visit. We are an ordinary couple paying one another a visit.

Now he asks, "What's the matter with you? Your voice sounds funny."

I explain that I have a cold (not true), and then admit that I have been crying (massively).

"Why?" he asks, greatly puzzled.

I am so relieved to see him, to be able to talk with him that I don't know where to begin. At last, I can pour out all of my fears and guilt.

"Because of all of the things I didn't do right," I quaver. I'm desperate to spill everything, afraid this chance to see him will soon be lost.

But now Jim looks confused and frowns a little, protesting, "Oh no," and making a gesture with his hand that says he isn't even thinking about such nonsense. As if to say, "What's the big deal? We said we were going to stay in touch, right?"

"They've moved me," he says instead, pleased and somewhat surprised, discussing his return to health and his present circumstances. "I'm going into the Second Angel's House." He indicates this is temporary. A test is going to be soon, and the coming weekend, he will be moved up again.

It sounds like the best, most wonderful place, far beyond human imagination.

I gaze at him, hungry to memorize every detail. Despite his wan appearance, his eyes are shining—his right eye somehow different, darker. As if looking into it would reveal worlds and worlds that I might enter.

* * *

I wake in a body that feels light as air, buoyant with awe, wonder, gratitude.

Intensely, vividly real Jim continues on. I have been sending love to him every night. *How have I missed that he has known, has sent love back, confirming me, accepting all of me, always?* I've been focused only on sending, and now realize that I have not been truly open to receiving. I've been visualizing Jim, but not allowing myself to trust and experience his consistent, present love for me.

It's true, I needed the anger—if only to break my pattern of trying to control and instead allow. I had not realized that I've become more and more rigid as the weeks have passed, having lost the flow and energy of the early days, and moved into "working" at being a good, spiritually attuned widow.

My practice could have evolved, have enabled me to be more present with what has been unfolding in me and between us. And yet, *hasn't it evolved?* It seems that trust is a practice which needs renewal as well.

What will I do with this gift of love plus a tender tutorial about getting back on the path? And why do I think I have to "do" anything?

I want to tell someone about what has happened to me, to let people know about Jim. But telling seems akin to draining the energy, complexity, and full import of my dream if I bring it into the harsh light of the everyday world.

I share with a few friends and family, but it's awkward and too big for us to hold.

Then I think of Quang.

QUANG SAYS NO

Obsession: A torment of wasteful energy
or an itch for an answer to rest your soul.

I'm excited to visit Quang again, which I am doing every few weeks while still taking his herbal medicines. When we sit down together, I tell him that I have finally seen Jim, remembering Quang's words at my first visit: "Let Jim go and he will come back to you." I am caught up in a sense of achievement and want his approval.

"Now," I proclaim, like a naive child, "I would like you to teach me how to see Jim on a regular basis, whenever I want!"

Quang is quick to correct me, although he is not unkind. "No," he says emphatically, "You don't want to do that. If you were to try to see him more often, it would not really be him; it would be a bad ghost!"

He shocks me when he says, "I keep a knife under my pillow in order to chase away any that come to me at night. Let Jim come as he will, but only once or twice a month at the most. Any more than that would be harmful and not really Jim."

I'm not frightened when I hear this, immediately considering that in his culture a ghost is not a cartoon or scary make-believe figure, but a powerful negative energy. I think that he is talking about the dangers of obsession. It's not an easily discounted label, like in our culture, though, more like a nightmare come to life or a kind of mental illness.

Of course. I feel stupid. Again, I have come up against my desire to control (instead of allowing), and Quang is telling me that if I do this I will be engaging with worlds and energy that I am barely beginning to understand. Much chastened, but accepting my ignorance and limitations, I return home with my bitter brew to drink.

Morning after: My new job is dealing with obsession, because in fact, I am practicing a version of it. I need to get control over my mental trash heap. *What else, besides the worries about failing Jim, am I obsessing about and why?* I keep rerunning painful memories of perceived failures and faults to do with family, friends, and my school community. I feel guilty because of the distance I am keeping from them.

Thus, I resolve to make an X on a piece of paper every time I have an unproductive or wasteful thought.

Evening: Twenty-eight times today I had a negative thought. I kept a tally all day. These thoughts ranged from fear about my future to neurotic imaginings (dramas with various characters) to guilt and sorrow (memories of Jim dying).

Clearly, taming obsession is going to take discipline and focus.

I decide to visualize the turquoise waves building and breaking on the sands of Iona when negativity takes over. Or to take some calming breaths and shift energy to my heart, sending some love instead to myself or Jim—or to any other person involved in my manufactured drama. Or I can divert the dark thoughts by turning on my creative engine and instead plan and dream about my writing.

Three days later: Thirteen times today I caught myself obsessing. I remain determined to cut out wasteful, unproductive thinking.

I tell Jim tonight that I'm feeling he is farther away, as I sense that his own path, apart from mine, is evolving where he is. I say that I too, am feeling like I'm moving more into the outer world and new projects. Yet, I don't want to lose the inner connection and the path I have set myself. *Practice, practice.*

When I send love to Jim, the candle flame leaps up high and bright.

SALT MINES

"For in grief, nothing 'stays put.' One keeps on emerging from a phase, but it always recurs. Round and round. Everything repeats. Am I going in circles or dare I hope that I am on a spiral?"
—*C.S. Lewis*

After my Real Jim dream, I'm realizing how much I'd been swamped with regrets. Jim's dismissal of the monster I'd been feeding is the biggest gift from that experience. But really, just as there is the issue of "poor me" that I address each night before bed in my practice—because that's my issue alone to deal with, it seems that regrets, disappointments, even resentments—whether about one's own failings or those of a loved one--are also in that category.

I'm working on the trap of obsession about such thoughts and feelings, but at the same time I'm enlarging my perspective.

So, this is what comes to me now: I think when two individuals first have a *karmic moment* (eyes meeting across a crowded room . . .) something is kindled that turns into the recognition of a destiny to live out together. That's a very pure moment, that spiritual spark. You meet that other soul, you fall in love, yes, but I believe there is something deeper and more mysterious also at work.

If you make a commitment, your journey together begins. Of course, the unprocessed emotional baggage that's come along with you inevitably begins to show up. It's individually owned, but it does get all mixed in with your lover's own unresolved issues. Sometimes its weight and influence can be eased or eliminated through the relationship, sometimes not. It's part of the journey, nevertheless. Unresolved issues can easily become the definition of the relationship, blurring the initial clarity about who sees you and whom you have also seen.

When the person you have journeyed with dies, I wish to believe that their baggage, insofar as it relates to you and the life you shared, also disappears. No more dragging around the blind pain and confusion from that life. After death, according to Rudolf Steiner and other traditions I've read, a soul spends a period of time doing a life review with their guardian angel. During this review, the soul has a direct experience of the effects on other people of one's actions and choices made in life. The positive choices are experienced as well as the negative ones.

Perhaps this time of transition is about shedding and learning. *Why else would it occur?*

After my Big Dream with Jim, his description about his move from one "angel house" to another felt connected with this process. It seems to me, therefore, that there is no more baggage on his end, because really, how could one imagine being in the spiritual realms with baggage? All gone, over with, done, leaving an ever-transforming soul that may have to repeat some lessons but is no longer entangled with working out a past relationship. With this perspective, I have decided that regrets are small things, like debris left on a road already traveled and no longer relevant for what now exists.

Certainly, we can't know how poor choices in life impact the soul in the spiritual worlds, but I feel that it's a mistake to express our worldly opinions. It's beyond anything we can imagine, it seems to me. And not being a religious scholar or saint, I am giving myself permission to riff on the matter!

Of course, my personal baggage is about feeling that I somehow failed to be "enough" to meet the enormity of Jim's death. I have felt guilty because I was not able to live up to my vision of my highest and best, baggage-free self.

But now, I believe that such tormented thoughts are a waste of time because there is no logical answer. There is heart work to be done, not head work. When I get caught in negative remnants of my past, I will have to remind myself how small-minded and limiting, that can be. *Why waste emotional energy, rather than growing into and nurturing what was originally seen so purely and is now the only truth?*

Furthermore, if Jim knows my heart, the "essential Me" in the way that I indeed experienced him after he died, why would he not have completely forgiven me for any times that I disappointed him? I believe this is why, when I saw him and spoke with him, he shook his head and said, "Oh, no." when I told him of my sorrows and regrets.

If I can know Jim's heart and let go of any of the unresolved feelings and disappointments that creep into any relationship (like yelling at him about abandonment during my meltdown) why wouldn't he be capable of doing the same for me?

NOT REALLY HERE?

*"What is time? The shadow on the dial, the striking
of the clock, the running of the sand, day and night,
summer and winter, months, years, centuries—
these are but arbitrary and outward signs, the measure
of Time, not of Time itself. Time is the Life of the soul."*
—*Henry Wadsworth Longfellow*

Yesterday I realized that I have been consistently forgetting to put the right date on a check. I always want to write "August." I suppose this is because my life as I knew it stopped in that month with Jim's seizure and the subsequent pronouncement of brain tumors.

I have said that Jim's watch stopped when he died. Since then, I can't get a watch to work on my wrist—I have bought two new ones and have had to return them.

I still often feel as if I'm caught in a strange dream from which I will soon awaken to find that life is normal again.

Maybe I'm not really here, but in between the worlds? Or maybe I'm not in between anything, because *in between* implies a known world and . . . what else? Maybe the shock of loss has peeled away my definition of reality, the one that has

143

been built by my family history, my culture, the language I speak, my community, my schooling, the books, and other media to which I've been exposed, my friends, the beliefs I've absorbed over my lifetime that have been my anchors for engagement in the time-bound world?

My soul is flowing through me timelessly—but now it seems to be boundless and free as I wander into an unknown future in an unfamiliar self, anchored here mostly by my seeking heart.

NOT YOUR FAIRY
GODMOTHER

"We can make ourselves weak or we can make ourselves strong. The amount of work is the same."
—Carlos Castaneda

I've begun (typical of me), to crowd my life with ordinary tasks and projects and I'm feeling very scattered. I feel on the threshold of a new life, with new thoughts, new commitments to stay focused and deepen my before-bed practice, more conscious of conserving my innocence about the import of my dreams and mystical experiences. For now, I generally regard them as mysterious gifts not ready to be brought, through conversation or writing, into the light of day.

I'm continuing to work on our house, which has walls that need plastering and minor carpentry throughout. I'm trying to do most of it myself—because I've always loved such work, but I've also hired someone to help me. I've also decided to share my home with T., a close friend who is warm and loving and a very busy person as a scenic artist and teacher. This means that we'll not get in one another's way too much. Her friendship and sense of humor and play is just what I need to help me create a social life without Jim, and her financial contribution will help slow down the shrinking of my bank account.

The garden book idea is taking shape and I can hardly believe my good fortune: Through a parent from the school, I have acquired a literary agent. She has moved up to our area from New York City, likes my vision, and is willing to take on my project if I can produce a good book proposal. I'm overwhelmed, awkward, and tongue-tied when we meet. I know nothing about how to write a proposal, but I'm determined to learn. I've also been in touch with my friend J., who is a book designer and packager for different print houses and she has offered to hire me for a proofreading job.

Thus, I found myself at her house for a week and being around her energy was intoxicating—even while I felt lonely and vulnerable not being home in my own safe space. *Baby steps*, I told myself. If I do a good job, says my friend, she will call me again. I figure helping birth books might lead to manifesting one of my own.

Back home again, I began my regular evening ritual to get centered and practice love and acceptance, and instead found myself crying for a long time.

True confessions: A good part of my distress was because I felt betrayed and abandoned. More truth: Well, I got a $72 speeding ticket and probably a $200 cracked windshield on my trip to J's house, which means all of those long hours feeling lonely and dying to be home were for naught. What I will earn from proofreading I must immediately spend.

I am now forced to recognize that I have been nursing a fantasy—that, from beyond, Jim was going to be protecting me from such negative events. My confidence in my path has been shattered and many sad and unproductive thoughts are crowding my mind. Should I give up pursuing my dreams and just grab whatever job comes my way?

After using up several tissues wrestling with feelings and facts, I finally figure it out. I can almost hear Jim explaining so kindly to my childish self: "I'm not your fairy godmother. I can't protect you from the laws of the world like getting traffic tickets. I'm a loving support for you, but I cannot work magic for such situations (although we could probably manifest a tow truck together if you ever need one). You have to accept that bad things will still happen to you, and you will need to find ways to deal with them.

"Know, however, that you are not alone."

PARADE OF HEARTS

March 20, spring equinox

I am lying in my bed in my family home.

There is a great fanfare outside, and the door to the fire escape by my room opens.

In comes a parade of high school students, all dressed like the playing cards in Alice in Wonderland.

Except that they are ALL HEARTS!

They all gather in a circle around my bed.

There is a celebratory air, a "surprise party" feel about them, a great sense of expectancy.

Then–TADA!–the line of kids by the door parts and through them, bounding up the stairs and into my room, is Jim.

"It's Jim!" I cry out, "It's Jim!"

This then, is the culmination and reason for the parade.

He comes over to me and takes my two hands so lovingly in his.

* * *

Joy wakes me.

I can still feel his touch.

JIM PAINTS ME

*"In a portrait, you always
leave part of yourself behind."*
—Mary Ellen Mark

4.15

I'm walking down Main Street in Brattleboro, heading towards
Ric Campman, a friend and one of the founders of River Gallery
Art School. He has asked to meet me, but I don't know why. As
I get close, I see him waiting on the sidewalk before the school.
Under his arm there is a rolled-up tube of paper, which he
hands to me, saying with the kindest of smiles that Jim, without
my knowledge, had come to the school in the early stages of his
illness, wanting to paint me. "But he was frustrated by the
outcome," says Ric, "and gave up, never taking his creation
home."

Jim often told me that he wanted to paint me—what more
wonderful and loving tribute? I bring the paper tube home and,
hands trembling, unroll it.

It is a very simple head-and-shoulders watercolor portrait:
me, with my long neck and a cloud of brilliant yellow hair.

From the upper right corner, a white dove descends, watching me.

Is that Jim, a promise for me always?

On the left side of the paper, a giraffe—my long-legged, somewhat ungainly animal symbol floats in space, with head cocked a bit humorously to look at me.

This, then, is the message Jim wanted to leave me, the image of me held in his heart over our too-brief years of knowing one another.

It's not the first time he made a portrait of me. And I of him as well. Our invite to our wedding was a simple handmade postcard that we illustrated together (which deeply embarrassed and angered my conventional father when he saw it). On the front, divided in two parts, we had each created a nude pen-and ink sketch of our betrothed. Not a cartoon or a caricature—a celebratory, but also somewhat serious sketch to share with friends and family, meant to symbolize what we saw in one another.

Jim drew me like a multiarmed Hindu deity, each hand holding a tool of creative expression: my fiddle, scrolls of paper, paintbrushes, pencils, pens, a trowel. I'm a whirling goddess of creative ferment.

I originally had drawn a three-quarter view of Jim following a path that led to a tall, shining building in the distance. I meant my sketch to depict the realization of his architectural vision.

When Jim saw what I'd created, I could tell he was disappointed and I was shaken to have failed. Did I not love as deeply and well, not see the true Jim?

I'm wondering now if he experienced it as a death picture. Was I having a premonition?

How do we think about premonitions in our culture? Do we dismiss them as the product of an overwrought imagination? A chronic depression that needs talk therapy and Prozac? Do we find an Indigenous healer who can do a soul retrieval? Or do we simply commit to growing our hearts and awareness, while trusting that all else will be as it should for this present life we are in?

There is no answer for such questions, but today I believe that premonitions are evidence of an innate spiritual capacity to know and understand much more about our life path than is presently accepted.

I tore up my first sketch of Jim and, after some quiet reflection, found another image. This time it worked: Above in the clouds, an angel stretches out a hand, sending a stream of brilliant light down into Jim's palms as he holds them out, kneeling before a ring of children dancing on the grass before him. He is speaking words of power into his palms and on his chest, there is a heart is glowing with love. I'm showing his life-dream to protect and nurture innocence in the world.

Instead of that first image of me that Jim drew, I am now holding the last. My throat aches as I look at it, my vision blurs.

Yes, there is a struggle to express a likeness, but oh! there is one part that has been given—more than any other—such deep attention and care.

Jim.

How lovingly, tenderly, and full you have painted my lips.

FINDING THE FIRE

*"Faith is the bird that feels the light and
sings when the dawn is still dark."*
—Rabindranath Tagore

4.30

I continue to feel tired and driven by all of my various creative challenges: the garden book proposal, the garden itself, work on the house, and my depleting bank account. I accepted notice from the "simplicity angels" for several months, but then stopped paying attention and now things feel even more scattered and out of control. I'm realizing I have to cut back on trying to complete the interior of the house. I long ago promised myself that I would not end up compromising my life in order to support the existence of a perfect dwelling, no matter how much I would love to finish and keep it. I do not, however, want it to become a shrine to the past. Even now, something is pushing me to explore beyond our valley.

About an hour ago, I was hobbling around the living room, halfheartedly cleaning up and complaining to myself about my aching feet. I began thinking about the relationship between my foot pain and my feelings about my life. It's fear. I'm once again afraid and reluctant to stand on my own, just as I was after Jim died. My feet curl away from the earth. I hold myself back from my willingness to be here. I'm forcing myself and thinking positively, but fundamentally I'm waiting to be rescued.

I shake myself all over and then begin to practice, like in the early days, walking consciously, with purpose, grasping the earth with my whole foot, feeling how the energy travels up my legs. It seems I endlessly have to pay attention to what my body is revealing about my inner life.

My lunar calendar says tomorrow is Beltane, the ancient Celtic festival on May 1 that marks the start of summer in Ireland and Scotland. I've planned a bonfire ceremony with six cherished women friends, and then I almost cancel because the weather is on the edge of wretched. But now I want warmth and ritual to herald the growth of new energy within, even as bright green spires in my garden are beginning to boldly emerge from the soil.

I call my friends and they come. We are up until 3:00 AM in a room illuminated by candlelight. Outside it is wet and frigid, but we are toasty. I put a big, fat candle on the floor in the middle of our circle to be our "fire." We dance, hug, share, and sing.

I am beginning to feel like a phoenix, I tell them.

I find myself saying that it's hard to be away from home for any period of time—because when I leave the safe, nurturing, and familiar, I experience myself as the "person I'm going to be." This is scary, but also stimulating, I admit.

So many experiences since Jim died have revealed that there is more to me than I will learn in this lifetime. And I continue to practice giving thanks for my many blessings. Still though, I return to the challenge of discernment: If I am going to accept being here, what will keep me here, open to what life brings, while moving in a direction that has purpose and meaning?

I am leaving soon to take a workshop about working with spiritual worlds. The teacher is a man named David Spangler. I don't remember when I first heard about him, but in my counterculture generation his name appeared as a key figure in the 1960's story of Findhorn, a coastal commune in northeastern Scotland with an astonishing garden that was renowned for producing giant-sized vegetables out of ground that was mostly sand. The secret ingredient, it seems, was the addition of help from nature spirits.

I fully embrace the Findhorn story because of my powerful connection with my own garden (not with the same results, however). There is that Roy Wilkinson quote I encountered during my visit to the Emerson College library in January: " *We see the physical world with the physical eye. To see the spiritual world, we need to develop a 'spiritual' eye.* "[1] By this time, the concept of invisible worlds and trusting the presence of wise and loving support is becoming more and more of a guiding story for me. My journey thus far has been quite solitary though, and I am hungry for fresh ideas and challenges.

David's history includes a mystical experience at age seven while in Morocco, when he felt himself merging with a timeless presence of Oneness within the cosmos, while simultaneously becoming aware of his choice to incarnate. Over the course of his life, he has become a mystic—studying, lecturing, learning from inner worlds of spirit, and acting as a clairvoyant channel for nonphysical entities.

His weekend workshop, "The Other Side of the Hedge: Working with Spiritual Worlds," is focused on learning about these entities, and includes working on our relationships with the dead. It's at a small retreat center in the Vermont hills, less than an hour away.

Who will come back home after?

THE OTHER SIDE OF
THE HEDGE

"Manifestation is an act of trust. It is the soul pouring itself out into its world, like a fisherman casting a net to gather in the fish he seeks; with each cast properly made, we will bring what we need to us, but first we must hurl ourselves into the depths without knowing just what lies beneath us."
—*David Spangler*

5.13

It's a cold, windy spring morning. The stovepipe is rattling as I leave the house, allowing the fire in the stove to die out. An hour's drive then to a retreat center west of me and an important new experience—the opportunity to learn and ask questions about my journey.

David turns out to be a warm, humorous man with a resonant voice and great kindness. No special guru clothing or jewelry. He is an ordinary comfort (this is a compliment), so present and grounded, ready to enjoy those of us who have shown up. *How does one become as inwardly light as he seems to be?*

I need his help. I've arrived here with all of my defenses up, nervous, ready to judge lest I be judged. My supposed positive growth from past months has disappeared and the old stiff habits of shyness and insecurity hang heavily on me. I am doing "awkward" very well.

Clearly, my feelings are shared by others in the group, and David solves the integration problem before all else. He pairs us off into circles of three, asking that we take a moment to close our eyes and get in touch with our heightened expectations for the weekend. "Open to the two who are sitting with you," he then says, "and feel glad to be with these two strangers who are not strangers. Fill the center of your circle with love. Send this same energy into the whole group."

Many thoughts run through my head when the exercise begins. *I don't have the energy for my two partners. I wish they looked more interesting.* (It hurts to write this now, admitting all of the old, critical, and fearful, as well as self-aggrandizing stuff that I drag around with me). The simple practice of sharing positive energy with them and with others, however, puts me in the right place. Of course, intention is everything. Heart work. I should have learned to do better by now. So far, I've only been sending love in my evening ritual to Jim.

In my journals, I keep writing about how shy and insecure I have been in my life, but now I'm starting to believe that, in a way, shyness is rather egotistical. I so often focus on myself in social encounters, instead of on the other person. Ugh. *How did I get to be so afraid of being seen? Haven't I by now had so many experiences that show me I deserve to be here?*

United, we open our eyes, more connected and ready to include one another.

David shares his understanding of *anam cara,* a Celtic phrase for "soul friend." These are inner guides or mentors that help us center ourselves whenever we come in contact with spiritual worlds—either through a practice or a revelation.

The deep beauty of this teaching is that these friends are not imagined spirits, but a special combination of inner qualities and gifts unique to each of us, which live deep in our souls. "Soul friends are your power," explains David. Thus, it is my beautiful, incarnated humanness that I celebrate and bring when I open to my inner wisdom.

For me, this teaching holds a big lesson in self-acceptance: "Focus on and trust what you can do, not what you wish were different."

No wonder David seems so grounded and clear.

How do I find my soul friends? I wonder. This comes next.

▲ DAVID'S EXERCISE ▲

Think of four attributes, special gifts you embody that empower you, which you consider part of how you know yourself, and which naturally manifest in ways that you express yourself in your life. For example, you may love to organize or may feel most connected to your essential self when you are in nature with your hands in the dirt. Or your creativity may ignite in the presence of children. Or perhaps you feel most "in your element" when you are in your kitchen, making delightful meals. Even ordinary, everyday tasks can evoke qualities in us that point to grounded inner knowing. Each attribute delivers infinite possibility.

———————

David counsels each of us to take until the next morning to find which four gifts best represent true aspects of our nature. It has been a day of sharing, kindness, and caring. In the middle of the night, I awake in my lower bunk, feeling as though something in me has turned a light on, and I find myself laughing.

In the morning, I make my list. Most of my words are nouns, but I also think of them as manifestations of living energies, like verbs: Nature. Rhythm. Imagination. Creativity. Dance. Music. Intuition. Resilience. Humor. Storytelling. Teaching.

Choosing four of these, I end up with: Nature, Music, Humor, and Creativity. I feel as though each, when active in me, inspires love, generosity, and gratitude.

In my journal, I write:

I feel loved in Nature, with all that she brings.
I feel connected in body, soul, and spirit when I express myself through sound and movement.

I feel grateful when I am able to unite people in laughter.

I feel grateful when I access a creative energy that brings something new into the world.

"Close your eyes," says Spangler when we are gathered again, "and imagine yourself surrounded by your four choices, symbolized however you wish—for example, as lights, or sounds, angelic beings, different colors, or spirit animals. Allow them to celebrate your wholeness. Stand then in your incarnated truth, which is not externally contrived, but embodied. Be your vibrant, empowered Self."

"Most of who you are," says David, "emerges from the Invisible. "Always, before you go on a soul journey, place yourself in your circle of power before you venture forth."

"Keep your priorities straight. *Even if you find yourself having amazing experiences on such journeys, ultimately, the good stuff is who you are, not how much phenomena you experience.*"

With this last sentence, I hear him telling me to be content to be ordinary, not a person with a superiority complex, setting herself apart from the muck and challenges of everyday life. A person who instead aims to bring her highest and best intentions into every encounter.

"Sometimes," David says, "the spiritual worlds are easily accessible. Other times, the channel is turned off. And that's fine. During those 'off' times, live your regular life without expectations or fears that anything has been lost."

"Just hang back and allow a cosmic reboot," I think he's saying.

It's delightful and deeply affirming to feel that a spiritual life can be a regular life—a life where there is laughter and lawn mowing, and even an obsession with *Star Trek*, if that's your thing. I also recognize the power of using imagination and intention to create an embodied, uncontrived experience. A soul friend could so easily be an abstract concept, but bringing my whole Self into acknowledging my innate inner qualities is truly the key. My heart practice with Jim grows because I don't "think" about it every night, I focus on my heart and intentionally feel the connection.

"Whenever you travel into other worlds, it is important to orient yourself in your personal power first," counsels David again, before he leads us on several guided inner journeys. Once again, I encounter the enigma of "allowing and intending." I allow images to flow through me with David's guidance, but the choices/intentions I make on the journey are intuitive, rather than forced or planned.

"Follow a track through a field and encounter a being that is deeply connected with your essential self," David might suggest. But he doesn't tell me that I will discover an extraordinarily beautiful white swan who will invite me to ride between its wings above a green and luminous landscape.

Such inner travels—and there are several journeys made throughout the weekend—are not simply entertaining diversions. How could they be when your starting point is your empowered soul? Instead, there seemed to be a process of confirmation in the give-and-receive in each journey: *This is you.*

And what about a relationship with the dead? David's teaching aligns with that of my Vietnamese healer, Quang. David teaches that the post-mortem state is veiled for the departed until familiarity is established with the new reality on the Other Side. After that, it is possible for our loved ones to return and be assistants (*but not fairy godmothers,* I remind myself).

I realize that this workshop has been a key experience for me.

When I thank David at the close of the weekend, he says, "Something shifted with your husband. I felt it." Yes. I have been well supported and guided. Have I really been muddling through only on my own or have I been assisted? *Of course! Silly question.*

I share my Iona stone with David before I leave. He smiles when he sees it, receives and cups it reverently in his hands like a dear friend, lowers his head, closes his eyes, and the two of them have a moment together.

No words, but another lesson, all the same.

A QUESTION OF NAMING

"It's a bizarre but wonderful feeling,
to arrive dead center of a target
you didn't even know you were aiming for."
—Lois McMaster Bujold

On Friday before I headed off for the Spangler workshop, there was a great wind and cold, a reminder of the bitter, endless winter days. In my home, the stovepipe rattled and banged, and the house shook in the gale. I pounded on the pipe to make sure that it would not fall out of the wall, then headed out. There was still a bit of fire in the stove.

Now I'm back home and David was right: there was a big shift in me after his workshop. I feel lighter and stronger now, in a way that I consider alchemical. It was not a matter of an adjustment in my thinking or logic, or in my attitudes. My insides were somehow rearranged and made more whole.

Moreover, there had also been a bit of a cosmic wrinkle at my home while I was away. On my return, my son, Marcus, met me at the front door with some extraordinary news.

On the day after my departure, the stovepipe was still rattling and banging when he and a friend had arrived to stay in my absence. Both remarked on the noise. But knowledge did not dawn until the body of the stove itself took up the sound and soot began to rhythmically puff out of the cracks. "There's something in there," said Marcus's friend, and left for home. Marcus got around to checking that evening and opened the door. A long, sharpish beak. A beady eye.

My stove had birthed a full-grown female merganser duck.

When my son finally came to terms with the reality of the situation (not quite comprehending how my stove, accessible only by four right angles of pipe and chimney and one three-inch-wide baffle, could contain such a creature), he described to me how he'd called his grandmother for advice. And then fetched a cardboard box and was able to reach in and lift the light, feathery, decidedly sooty, and exhausted duck from the ashes, and place her therein for the night. In the morning, he showed her the pond by the river. She quacked for joy, he reported, and took a swim, and since then had been napping on the edge of the water.

I'm standing with my mouth open at the door, hearing this, and then Marcus pointed to the riverbank. I ran over to the edge of the river, and as I arrived, the duck calmly slipped into the clear water and swooped off downstream while I watched in amazement.

Had the poor creature been blown down in the gale and somehow found her way into the stove, which, by the way, was not yet cold when I left?

Or was there another explanation?

There had to be a message for me in this strange event—I was convinced beyond a doubt. But what was it?!

I woke around 3 AM, almost exclaiming aloud as I sat up, grabbed my pen and journal, and wrote this letter:

Dear Jim,

You know I look for messages from the cosmos all the time, especially now that you are gone. No, I do not think you paid your former home a visit in duck form (although remembering your sense of humor, I wouldn't put it past you). No, it's taken me until this moment, three o'clock in the morning to figure it out.

It may have looked like a duck, but it was really a phoenix!

Out in the yard, all of the daffodils the children planted for you last autumn are up and leaping and trumpeting on the riverbank. The river melted gently this year, no torrents of water, nor chunks of ice on the edges, and now it's round-the-clock work is to remind me about flow. "Be a duck," it murmurs now, outside in the remnants of night, wanting to share in the mystery or reclaim one of its symbols.

Everywhere I go these days, I meet or hear about someone struggling with or dying of cancer. There is a battle waged, but I remember well that point when the battle metamorphoses and the terrain becomes pregnant with stillness, peace, and possibility. Love emerges, both in the warrior and in those who also have held the sword.

Those who find some key to unlock a door into new life here, find they have acquired a brimming, transformative energy that comes from the conquering of fear. Energy which cannot be held, but must be shared. And you, Jim, for whom the other door opened, still find so many beautiful ways to send that energy back.

If I meet someone new to the kind of pain and process that I am going through, there is always an element of excitement in me, strange to say. "Wait," I often share, "watch and stay open because amazing things will come your way. More love and grace than you ever would have dreamed possible. Light a candle every night and cry if you need to, but don't forget to ask for help. Write down your dreams. Do at least one thing you have been talking all your life because you will find much is possible.

"Something wonderful will hold you.

"And if by chance a big wind gets too full of itself and throws you down, say, a chimney, and you have to crawl through smoke and soot in the dark, just remember: A door will open.

"Say: 'I may look like a duck, but can't you tell? I'm a phoenix.'"

The letter sits on my desk for several weeks. And then, I think of the schoolchildren and their families who loved us. I have not been in touch with them since Jim's memorial service because I've not been ready, have not even known what to share. Now, I decide the letter has a purpose—it's a message both from me—and from Jim.

I put the letter in a brown envelope and send it off to the editor of our local paper, feeling vulnerable, but also heart-high and ready.

Of course, a skeptic will ask how it is possible for a duck to show up in my stove! I will ponder this in days ahead. There will be more than one answer, I am sure, but the most important one, I'd say, has already been revealed.

INTERWOVEN, ALL
THE SAME

*"Vital lives are about action. You can't feel warmth
unless you create it, can't feel delight until you play,
can't know serendipity unless you risk."*
—Joan M. Erickson

6.12

My phoenix letter appeared in the newspaper today—my first
published piece. I was overwhelmed when I saw it. Since I have
not had any connection with our school community, I wished
to let everyone know that I/we are okay, and that Jim's spirit
and energy continues on. It did feel awkward, however, being
so public about my journey. *Might I be judged a raving widow,
hiding out in her house, and deluding herself with wild visions
and pretensions?*

It's hard to write about my journey without sounding gushy
or maudlin or trite. In *A Grief Observed,* C.S. Lewis describes
his experience of a contact, a sound, from the other side by
saying: "One moment last night can be described in similes;
otherwise, it won't go into language at all."[1] This was a man
who knew that the feeling he experienced was so otherworldly

that to try to express the whole of it risked reducing its power to something small and cheap.

I too acknowledge this struggle.

Despite my fears, I muster up the courage to contact the newspaper editor and ask if I might be able to contribute other pieces for the paper. He responds by suggesting that perhaps I would like to write an occasional column. I'm stunned. The phoenix rises!

Now, there is another inner challenge. It's not about the positive responses to my writing—and there are many that come my way from friends, and strangers too. It's much bigger than that. I am coming to realize that, were I given the opportunity to turn back the clock and have Jim restored to me, and everything just the way it once was, it would be very hard to choose. I truly cannot imagine erasing all that has happened inside me since Jim died.

Because I feel that I am more Rondi than I have ever been.

And would Jim ask it of me? Every sense that I have had of him is that, in the spiritual worlds, there is only our individual unfolding, unattached to the choices or destiny of relationships in a former life.

Unattached, yes. But I want to say "interwoven," all the same. It's like my dream a few nights before Beltane, when Jim and a whole crowd of teenagers dressed like hearts on a pack of cards marched into my bedroom to visit me. There were two joys: One was to experience Jim—his humor and love. The other was that I felt deeply happy to see him hanging out with teenagers. When we shared the kindergarten, he often said that he felt his real mission was to work with that age group. Now, it seems as though he is.

Perhaps we are both in the same place, answering the same question: just not in the way I originally thought we were. Maybe we are not asking, "Who am I without my beloved in my life?" But "Who am I *with* my beloved, beyond time."

We are not attached, in a worldly sense. Not living as though frozen in the past, but each transforming, in the highest spiritual sense.

Here I am, my striving, evolving self, more than ever before. And at the same time with a growing awareness of belonging to infinite expressions of a greater whole.

THE THIRD QUESTION

SPIRIT

WHAT IS MY SOURCE
OF STRENGTH?

A LIVING PRESENCE

"The gloom of the world is but a shadow;
Behind it, yet within our reach, there is joy.
There is radiance and glory in the darkness, could we but see,
And to see, we have only to look."
—Friar Giovanni Giocondo (1433–1515)

I've memorized part of Friar Giovanni Giocondo's vivid assertion of the power and beauty underlying our shadowed, suffering world. I often recite it as part of my ritual before bed.

Giocondo ends by passionately declaring:

Life is so full of meaning and purpose, so full of beauty beneath its covering, that you will find earth but cloaks your heaven. Courage then to claim it; that is all! But courage you have, and the knowledge that we are pilgrims together, wending through unknown country, home.

Giocondo's message inspires tonight while considering a David Spangler question from his workshop, "What does the sacred represent for you?"

What do I experience as transcendent, an ultimate quality or truth, inviolate, boundless, and sacrosanct?

What comes to me first is an awareness of our land and the river—and with this realization, there comes something new. I'm sitting by an open window, the air smells of summer, and outside in the dark, Nature becomes, in Giocondo's words, a "living presence, woven of love, by wisdom, with power." I feel myself extended out, interconnected: My awareness, my senses, even the edges of my body, have all been absorbed into our valley, the night, our garden, the sleeping animals, the nighttime hunters, birds, bugs, and stars. It's a moment of infinity, brief and electric.

I sit quietly for a long time afterward. To be loved and known. Not only known, but knowing. Not *sacred* defined as something outside myself, but *being so*.

When I was in my early twenties, I remember hungering for such an experience of merging while walking on a stretch of wild beach in Maine. Everything was there for me—an infinite, cloudless blue sky, surf foaming over stones and sand, sharp, salty air—and yet nothing stirred within. I felt the emptiness like a mystery in my soul that was waiting to be resolved.

I was not a deprived or unhappy child, just still unborn in some ways. I had no depth to plumb, nothing that could resonate with the wind and pulse of the sea. I had not truly loved or lost, or suffered.

Tonight, I think: *Strange how a soul can be virginal, unopened, because it has not yet moved.* Tonight, I understand Giocondo's words, "radiance and glory in the darkness, could we but see."

Does it take suffering to know this? Tonight, I've known sacredness, experienced so briefly how I am woven into Nature's infinite tapestry of life.

What is the connection between love and sacredness? Since losing Jim, I keep thinking about my capacity to love. I have been loved in my life, and yet maybe there is something in me, *or has been* something in me, still asleep. I'm thinking of my numb heart, when a younger me was walking by the ocean in Maine. How can I experience sacredness if I've not plumbed the depths of love? Is love awakened the seed for growing a greater awareness of connection to the whole?

There was that time, in a month near the end of the final year at our little school, when I became suddenly, acutely aware of Jim moving about our kindergarten classroom. He was cleaning up as I was resting from a morning spent playing and sharing with twenty exuberant five- and six-year-olds.

In that moment, I felt such an aching lift in my heart as I watched him, and I knew that I was feeling something deeper for him than I had ever felt before. My heart yearned for him and all he was in my life.

In that moment, I believe I was experiencing the full scope of our history together, like a life panorama before life is lost.

These days, when I practice my evening ritual of sending love to Jim, I still must consciously focus on my heart to ensure that my practice is energized by an authentic, empowered intention. When I get it right, my soul is flooded with a full awareness of his being. Even after months of practice, it still takes discipline to bring the whole of myself to that space. I love to get inside my head and too often bypass my heart, eager to push on to the next idea or task, whatever it might be. It's so easy to fall into abstraction and lose the living energy. I do this practice, but I get scattered. I rebel. I become bored with it. I feel guilty.

Yet, I know I am changing.

But still. Still. I fall into taking my blessings for granted.

"Maybe your wisdom tooth needs to come out!" I yell in a dream at a woman who is complaining of a hearing problem.

During a recent visit with friends, I found myself making a surprising statement about what I've been learning: If I commit to working with spiritual worlds, I unequivocally must let go of naysaying. I feel now as though I am developing a new organ of perception, a sense of inner equanimity and caring.

It's not possible to practice love, acceptance, and gratitude before bed every night without feeling acutely how negativity can cause pain in a tender, evolving self.

Thus: *Isn't this brightening core in me, a growing power of loving and being loved, a source of strength?*

LET THERE BE GIANTS

7.10

Jim is back and he is well!

And he has grown very tall.

"You must be at least six-foot-eight!" I exclaim, leaning back, looking up to see all of him.

We walk down a path, side by side, and I put my arm around him.

My arm goes around his knees!

He explains that he has been helped to grow, at last, to his correct height.

He turns toward me, looks down at me.

I look up at his serious, beautiful face.

In our eyes, acknowledgment and understanding.

SOURCE OF STRENGTH

"What we know is not much.
What we do not know is immense. "
–Pierre-Simon, marquis de Laplace

If I lost everything now, including family, friends, home, health, and physical capacity, what, if anything, would keep me going? What makes a flower pick growing through a crack in asphalt as a goal in life? I think it's tough to answer where most people find their strength, myself included.

For some, there could be an unshakeable connection with a belief system, religion, or life philosophy. Or it could come from a cultural identity born out of years of tradition—being Jewish comes to mind. Or from an ancestral fight for survival in the face of unrelenting odds, such as the Native American and African American peoples have faced throughout history. A family story that is told over and over, down through the generations, could teach a person courage. *We don't give up.*

I have to look back to see what has sustained me and made me resilient up to now, realizing that I have not lost everything. Still, losing Jim has been hard enough that I really want to go deeper and ask myself why I'm still here.

As I look back to the time when I first took up an old journal and started to keep a record, nearly a year ago, while Jim was dying, I can see how pen and paper have befriended me with attentive, nonjudgmental companionship. The discipline has given me stability over the months, as well as space for self-reflection. This brings me now to think about the three big challenges to my healing from loss. They've created the structure of my story.

Body. Soul. Spirit. I accept by now that, for me, healing from loss has had to be a spiritual path. A real path, with trials and roadblocks and hard lessons.

It began with my body and how it handled stress.

Jim died. *Will grief kill me?* I wondered. I ached all over. My heart hurt and pounded wildly and erratically at times. I found it hard to breathe, hard to sleep, hard to think. Was the physical part of me going to hold together, especially because the stress had actually started many months earlier?

There are many natural approaches to healing a body that has been under great stress. I continue to explore them, from Quang's medicine to yoga and energy work to the therapy of massive house and yard cleaning. Even getting a haircut helps.

And while I was needing to focus on the body issues, with Quang's help and the anchoring nightly practice of love and acceptance, I still had to be dealing with my soul without its mate, lost and wandering through heavy dreams, fears, and longings.

My soul was asking: *Who am I without my beloved? Who will understand and love me now? Do I have a right to be here, or a reason or purpose?*

The way to heal my soul has been through creativity and self-expression. The act of keeping a journal eventually brought a life dream to the surface: the goal of creating a writing career.

It hasn't been simple though, but planning has been key. Mammy knew what she was talking about when during the hardest of times she told me, "Just keep walking."

For me, it's not only the step-after-step, day-after-day way out of the labyrinth of sorrow. It's also been the increasing awareness that the more I dare, the more I recover and build anew. And, as I wrote before, I finally have discovered that I am "more Rondi than I've ever been."

Who will love me? First, I will love myself.

I guess what I'm saying is that grief has shown me not only what I am made of, but also what I might dream of becoming.

And I find that there's no need to solve my whole life and put everything that fell apart back together. The practice of trust and acceptance has become the antidote for despair. I'm trusting that I will find my way, and I accept that if I go down the wrong path, I will be shown what to do next.

So that's been my soul's recovery up to now. But this third challenge hits at the very deepest level: Spirit: *What is my source of strength?*

Does my source of strength come from knowing where I'm lacking and not giving up the search for a deep comfort in my heart and soul when I get it right? I find the better I know myself and what nurtures my spirit, the more I become my highest and best. And have the strength to deal with whatever life brings.

My cultural roots contain a streak of rebellion. I'm a Dutch immigrant farmer's granddaughter with the blood of Swedish and Norwegian immigrants in her veins as well. In the 1800s, my mother's father immigrated to a Minnesota farming county in order to be free of the rigid dictums of the Dutch Reform Church back home in Holland. His favorite quote was:

Man is his own star, and the soul that can
Render an honest and a perfect man,
Commands all light, all influence, all fate . . .

My grandfather also refused to join the local church. My mother told of stones being thrown at her and her sisters by other children on the mile-long walk to the local one-room schoolhouse because they did not attend religious services.

My father was not one to belong to established religions either; nevertheless, we children knew he had been sickly and even near death in childhood. The teachings of Unity Church and Christian Science when young eventually led to a sudden healing at age thirty-three. . He was ever after committed to a philosophy of mind over matter, nurturing a dream of founding a college where he could share the bounty of a life spent in study of the Bible and Platonic educational philosophy. He loved his children and was gifted and inspiring, but he was not a practical man. There were two periods of time when he withdrew from the family and prayed in solitude for God to deliver some needed cash, while Mom either sold something valuable or went out and got a job.

We kids were fortunate: There was deep love between our parents without a doubt, and this was reflected in our experience of family; although after Dad died, Mom declared, "When I get to heaven and see him, I'm going to run and throw my arms around him. And then I'm going to give him a piece of my mind."

We children were thus poised between the studious, Christian, often heavily didactic passions of our father, and the agnostic, unfailing devotion, and generosity of our mother. Dad was driven to teach and elevate. Mom was most fulfilled when she could feed and nurture.

I believe now that I have solved what felt like a disharmony in their relationship by insisting that in my own life, I will always find my way through my own experiences and interpretations. This commitment is both stubborn and pushes me into new and exciting territory at times. Sometimes it makes life a lot more complicated.

My father introduced me to Viktor Frankl's book *Man's Search for Meaning* when I was a teenager. Frankl was an acclaimed Austrian psychiatrist and concentration camp survivor who, while he was incarcerated in Auschwitz, maintained his will to live by keeping a shining life purpose ahead of him. His goal for when he was free again was the completion of a manuscript he had been working on before his capture. His other anchor was an inner image of his beloved wife and the awareness that his love for her was beyond the physical and found its roots in the spiritual and eternal.

He wrote:

Love goes very far beyond the physical person of the beloved. It finds its deepest meaning in his spiritual being, his inner self. Whether or not he is actually present, whether or not he is still alive at all, ceases somehow to be of importance.

In fact, Frankl's wife had already died in a concentration camp, which makes me consider the ways in which she, in fact, might have been giving him love and strength from the Other Side during that time.

Knowledge of love beyond the physical (which certainly had become part of my evening practice) is a source of strength too. *How might this be related to my question about the will that keeps a person from giving up? Can my source of strength be more than just tenacity?* I have wondered.

For almost three years before I met Jim, I was committed to a practice of Transcendental Meditation. It was not easy to shut my bedroom door on my young children twice a day and claim twenty minutes for myself. But every now and then, the discipline would bring me to a level of deepest peace and inner calm.

I realized at those times that if I were able to sustain such calm I could withstand anything. I felt able to understand how a monk could light himself on fire, without fear, simply letting go of life without clinging. Suffering existed somewhere, but not where he was.

I also got a sense of this, I realize now, when I committed to natural childbirth in the Sixties. I practiced breathing and visualizing as instructed. I also patiently corrected the elderly nurse when I was in labor and she asked, "How are your pains, dear?"

"They are not *pains,*" I declared through gritted teeth, "They are contractions." I also remember keeping my consciousness on a high shelf, divorcing myself from my body while doing the hard work of pushing.

I've always been inspired by tales of the great explorers who put themselves through incredible suffering in order to fulfill a goal like reaching the North Pole or the South Pole, climbing Mount Everest, and sailing alone around the world. Women adventurers, as well, and those who stood up for what was right like the heroic suffragettes who fought for women's right to vote and Harriet Tubman, who led hundreds of slaves to freedom. And let's be honest: We countless, unsung, heroic women who choose suffering and risk death every time we give birth also deserve a mention.

My history with practicing meditation and natural childbirth seems to have been about a desire for self-mastery when confronting the dark power of pain and fear.

Is this what has driven my choices? The willingness in me, the hunger even, to face the unknown, with the knowledge that afterwards I will never be the same? If this is true for me, I'm sure I'm not unique. Isn't that a key source of strength, the longing for transformation of self?

As the summer begins to head into another autumn, the time when the Unthinkable happened, I have to say what for me now feels obvious, that being able to give and receive love as a spiritual practice has become an ultimate source.

Would it sustain me if I lost everything—and I mean, everything? How would life appear to me without my community, my home, family, friends, health—all of those interweaving energies?

If my body and mind were able at all to function, if I still could connect with my creative spirit, I hope I would still be able to find a source of strength and purpose for living.

Ultimately though, it would have to be acts of love that would sustain me. Not in the intimate way I have been fortunate to know--how the smallest hint of love's infinite power might be known in a relationship. I'm imagining Love as its own Universe—vibrant, oceanic. An endless resource for the heart to draw from.

If I were able to reach such a place in myself, it would be a greater source of strength than anything else that I can think of.

When speaking of tragedy, the German psychotherapist Bert Hellinger once said, "Suffering gives the soul more weight."

There are those few who get to live lightly on the earth, but for most of humanity, a time comes when we have to confront what we are made of. This is okay with me. "Poems amount to so little when you write them too early in your life," wrote the poet Rainier Marie Rilke.

Let this then be the goal of my life, to become a good poem. A life of insight, compassion, and promise all compressed into a few, tenderly realized truths!

AUGUST TENTH

Always Jim

Two nights after our wedding, careful not to wake Jim, I slipped silently from our bed and stepped outside to wander in the dark, wrapped only in a blanket. I was in an agony of fear that I had made a terrible mistake, that Jim could not possibly love me, that another woman would take him away from me, and now I was bound to him and inextricably heading for a future of hurt and loss.

I was also saying goodbye to my hard-won freedom after a very difficult divorce. Perhaps too, this was another premonition of the terrible work of his dying that lay ahead.

When I look back, what would I change? The inner conflict. Why wander around in the dark? Why not simply wake the man I just married and get some reassurance? My fear of fully opening and trusting a new relationship no doubt deprived us of joy at some of our most precious moments together.

On our tenth wedding anniversary, I decide to spend the afternoon on the high bank along the Connecticut River where we were married. It is a warm, late summer day. I park my car above a big hayfield, cross some railroad tracks, and as I begin to walk through the tall grass towards a level shelf of land under trees by the water, I realize that I've slipped into that haunted state of mind that occurs with the revisiting of a strong memory.

The scene is empty and quiet now, no crowds of friends, no running, laughing children, no Jim with his loving look. The river is sparkling, and the trees are rustling with a soft breeze.

I find the same intimate green space on the high riverbank under big old maple trees, and stop first to stand in the place before the fallen poplar where we stood and spoke our vows. The air is charged with memories but I do not feel like crying. It's peaceful here.

I move to sit in the grass on the edge of the bank above the river, and begin to eat a sandwich I've brought along. The bank is about twenty feet high, and I cannot see the water's edge below. An osprey circles above the water, calls out three times, and then three times again, and then again three times before heading downriver.

I know I am looking for some sign from Jim, and my heart yearns out into the broad expanse of the Connecticut River that stretches from here in Vermont across to the far New Hampshire shore. I sit for a while, then close my eyes and try to visualize the whole of Jim, especially his face. I grow very calm.

And then, I hear a chorus of quacking.

I open my eyes, and directly below me, a large, dark shape is moving out from the bank into the river. Not one, but a flotilla of ten young merganser ducks, swimming in formation, all quacking away! I verify the count as they swim upriver. *Ten for our tenth anniversary on August tenth?*

Jim speaks *merganser*. Is there not a conjuring here with our beloved wild ducks?

No delicate butterflies landing on my shoulders, no ruby-throated hummingbirds, no rainbows. The perfect choice for us, no second-guessing required. *I get it, Jim!*

When we were first dating: greedy for romance, I hinted that it would be lovely to receive some flowers.

Jim had smiled and said nothing. And it was spring.

Two days later, a flower delivery truck pulled up in front of my home and two or three daffodils were formally delivered. And the day after that, several more. Daffodils kept coming, all week, at first a tentative announcement and then, over time, an energetic crowd, just the way they emerge every spring to finally wash across fresh, new grass in a golden wave. They crowded my desk by the weekend, a golden chorus shouting joyfully about me.

I get it, Jim! With a quacking Merganser Parade on this otherwise lonely anniversary, I'm laughing and calling out my thanks, with a promise to remember.

The wind rises then, blows and lifts into the tops of the trees, which toss, bend, and dance.

EVEN DEATH

I'm lying on my back, asleep. And here, like so many slow-burning memories past midnight, is Jim.

He settles on top of me. He almost enters me.

The problem of not-quite begins to surface in me; I want to urge him forward. But he's teasing me, digging his fingers into my ribs. It sort of tickles, sort of hurts.

"Get on with it," I think I'll say to him, so grateful that he's here, but why the teasing? I feel his head next to mine and reach up to caress his soft hair.

But he's bald. Ah yes, he's ill, *I remember. But that's okay; I open myself even more to him. And yet, he persists in not moving, just poking me in the ribs with his bony fingers, not poking me elsewhere.*

I finally push his head back so I can really look at him, laugh at his teasing.

His face is a grinning skull!

Strangely, I am neither shocked nor afraid. Even so, I immediately begin to make the sign of the cross, intoning the Lord's Prayer.

Then he melts away and my body is empty.

* * *

And I open my eyes.

I think two thoughts. First: *Why did I, in the spiritual-but-not-religious camp, have such a patently Catholic response?*

Second and more important: *I had no fear!*

I can even love Jim's skeleton self.

DIVINATION

"When you really want something,
the universe always conspires in your favor."
—Paulo Coelho

7.15

For a brief time after Jim's first doctor advised us to call hospice, Jim joined a cancer support group. There, he received the name of a psychic, a woman who channeled a spirit guide named Careen. We'd never even heard of consulting a channeler before, but she came highly recommended by other members of his group, so we made an appointment.

We traveled north to a remote Vermont valley that led to a dirt road snaking up into the hills, then another dirt road, and finally, fields, flowers, and a lovely home full of art and smiling Jacqueline, with an invite to sit on her couch.

There was no mumbo-jumbo involved. Jacqueline closed her eyes, we all slowed down, and then, after a few moments, someone else was there. Her face and posture seemed to transform into a smaller, more compact elder who was a warm, humorous, life-affirming being. Because the person who was the host was sitting with her eyes closed, making space for this other, the session seemed intensely private, even interiorized. Defenses were left behind. We spoke out of our hearts.

In some way, it felt like dowsing. The answers were there—had always been there—inside us. The entity known as Careen just reminded us of what we already knew.

Careen did not play on our emotions with elaborate scenarios of future lives together or past lives played out. He expanded our knowledge of what a life can be.

We had been stuck in the tragedy and terrors of our unexpected life crisis. Careen helped us to remember that the soul is much greater than a spark temporarily trapped in a closet. "A soul is something shining, eternal," he said.

Yes, of course. Just the gift of being reminded to change the focus. Death is not failure; death can be your best work. Yes, we would have to contend with pain and confusion in the future and a tremendous Unknown. But remembering to focus on what is eternal could give us comfort during the hard times ahead.

Perhaps the most significant gift from Careen came when Jim asked about Mammy. He was tormented with thoughts about how his passing would hit her hard, and conflicted with guilt over how much of her life she had sacrificed for him. He felt therefore that she would never have the life she was born for and deserved.

Careen was almost stern when he answered, "Your mother is so much more than you can ever imagine! Let go of limiting her in your thinking."

It is so easy to fall into this trap in relationships, I thought after. *Do I consistently see potential or do I more often focus about limitations? Do I live a life of trusting or of fearing?*

I'm thinking about our time with Careen as I drive to northern Vermont to attend an annual dowsing conference. It was Dr. L. who gave me a pendulum as a tool to help me make the intuitive choices about Jim's care, since I was mostly on my own except for a visit from a hospice caregiver twice a week.

After learning, while nursing Jim, that we have the capacity to know and feel something invisible, I've been on a path to learn more about other dimensions of human potential on the deepest level possible. I've explored energy healing, divination, manifestation, and dreamwork. I've learned about casting Celtic runestones and reading tarot cards, and about using dowsing rods on my land to track currents of water underground. This summer, I discovered the Silva Mind Control method in a book at a friend's house and added a new practice to my usual bedtime ritual. I am working on manifesting a writing career. I count backwards from one hundred. With each number, I visualize myself taking a step further down a long stairway that leads underground. Deeper and deeper, I go, until at last, I arrive in a beautiful garden. There, growing from the good earth, are all of the books I am planning to write. Intention, energy, programmed and planted in my consciousness. I understand that the more real I can make my goal, the more its energy begins to transform into reality.

I've taken a big step above ground as well: before I left for the dowsing conference, I put my garden book proposal in the mail. Time to give thanks to all of my helpers, seen and unseen. Will my dream come true?

I do realize that I've either done a good job or not, and that will determine its success. I'm a new writer. No fairy godmother stuff—I ready myself to accept the possibility of disappointment, not as an obstacle, however, but as a corrective guidepost on the path to my ultimate goal.

I arrive at the conference, but as usual, my mind is too scattered to make much of what is being presented, which is typical of me this year. What does seem portentous, however, is a connection I make with a woman named April Frost, who sits on the lawn near me at lunchtime. April shares that she is part Native American and has been involved with animals all of her life. She tells me that she is a dog trainer who has developed a new method of training that uses visualization and heart work (very like my evening ritual of sending love to Jim!) as a powerful method for connecting with any animal. Animals— especially dogs, she says—recognize intention and emotion more than any other form of communication.

There is that word again: *intention.* I sense there is something to learn from her.

Strange to say, I've had a dream about dogs in the past month. I like dogs, but have never had one or particularly wished for one. So, why that memorable dream a few weeks ago that contained a very big hill with hundreds of dogs running pell-mell down its sides?

April tells me that her life turned around after she got Lyme disease. She was too ill to teach her regular dog training classes and was in danger of losing her home. Then she happened to be conducting a private training lesson with a woman who earned her living as a psychic. April got around to sharing her struggles and the woman had looked at her and asked if she believed her dogs had spiritual power. "Of course," April had replied.

"Then why haven't you asked them to help you?" asked the woman.

April said she was stunned at the thought. But that night, she went out under the stars and cried aloud, "I need help!"

From that time forward, her life began to turn around, she told me. She was able to cure her Lyme disease. New clients flooded in, excited to learn about her unique training method that she was beginning to share widely.

April's story of the realization of her dreams has me inspired. I've been wondering whether I am going to get some sort of rude awakening, since I am still hanging around waiting for my writing career dream to manifest.

Does life really work that way? I am in a financial hole. I could get a nice, safe job, but I rebel. I am not ready to go back to normal. So, what am I doing, really? I'm testing out a new way of being, trying to trust the lessons and gifts that are coming my way. I am trying to allow the energy of a new me to be born, the realization of a creative new life to emerge, while continuing to focus clearly on what I want that life to look like.

Maybe all I really need to do is to stand outside in my garden and yell, "I need help!"

IF YOU CAN SEE IT

*"Resolute imagination is the beginning
of all magical operations."
—Paracelsus*

9.17

I've headed off to Colorado to meet Kyra and journey back to my home in Vermont with her and her horse Ffynnon Garw (a Welsh name—she just calls him Speedy). As much as she loves the West, her dream is to compete on a level that is not available in that cowboy culture part of the country. I'm excited to be able to spend some real time with her. It's another adventure, plus we've barely connected since Jim died.

I'm also wondering if I will be able to find to way to share a bit about some of the things I've learned over the months. I plan to tell her about how I am visualizing a garden of books sprouting out of soil well fertilized with hopes and dreams.

There is lots of time for good conversation in the truck as we head East. Rainbows chase us across. And all the way, we practice manifesting. It's a perfect opportunity and, of course, as far as the horse and trailer combo goes, we have an interesting challenge to practice with. It's about how to manifest a parking space for our overnights. Motels don't generally welcome people with horses and big horse trailers so we need to find generous souls who will take us in. We are in a great groove: Time after time, we pull into a town, ask at a gas station or general store, and in a short time, we are bedded down at someone's ranch or mini farm and have made new friends.

We also work on manifesting a job for Kyra. She dreams of finding a lovely New England farm owned by kind people who welcome her expertise as a horse trainer and who can afford to do things well. We visualize their numerous lovely, well-bred horses, which she will train, ride, and show. We see a big barn with an elegant stall for her horse and nearby, a charming little dwelling for her. There is also a big enough salary to support high-level competition with her horse and the other horses as well.

"Health insurance," I add.

We arrive in Vermont at last, pull into my yard and let Speedy out to graze. Then, we check the local paper.

And there's the job! A New Hampshire politician and his wife have a Morgan horse farm and they are looking for someone to manage the operation. There's a house for Kyra, a stall for her horse. A great salary. *Health insurance.*

Kyra is the only person to apply. She is hired immediately.

Coincidentally, her new home happens to be in the same town as spiritual dog trainer April Frost, my acquaintance from the dowsing conference.

Little do I know how significant this will become.

CAT CONSPIRACY

"I was here all along."
– Cinder the Cat

Ten days after I'm back in Vermont, I wake on my birthday with no small degree of anticipation. Surely, I will be feted in some special way—by family, friends, definitely Jim. I am wondering if perhaps I will hear about the garden book proposal, which I'd put in the mail more than a month ago. It could be a cosmic birthday present.

Hubris. It turns out to be a long, lonely day, with little to confirm me. All of my friends and relatives seem to be busy, and although there are a few loving phone calls, I head upstairs for bed in the evening feeling quite deflated. I sit before my altar without engagement or focus, close my eyes and try to summon up some acceptance and gratitude for being on the earth at age forty-nine without a definite future. But the lights remain off inside.

Our black cat, Cinder, is purring, rubbing, and leaning against my back, then leaning on my right arm. I caress her without acknowledging her attention, still lost in self-pity. No one has even given me a present or sent a card today. *Where do*

I exist? Who cares that I live? Cinder rubs against me now, on my other side, insistent. I shake myself a little and sigh, open my eyes and gaze absently down at the top of my altar.

And blink in disbelief.

There, placed ceremoniously in the center, lies a nice, big, fat mouse. I burst into laughter while Cinder, delighted that her offering has been accepted, increases the throb of her purring.

The gift of laughter is the only present I receive that day.

WILD GEESE

My life, like a span of geese,
Gathers each night at your door . . .

10.12

My stomach jumps as I write this date in my journal, one month before the anniversary of Jim's death. *Why am I so caught in anticipation? What do I think will happen?* I can feel a thrum of pain on the edges of consciousness, a heavy wheel of memory is rolling inexorably towards my heart.

I'm awakened in the middle of the night by the sound of a great many wild geese flying over the house. I cannot at first identify what is happening—I came out of sleep believing I'd heard voices calling outside in the dark. It must have been a huge flock.

I yearn to join them. Wild geese, calling in the night—I think then of a love poem I call "Gathering" that I wrote to Jim two years before he died.

The poem arrived so that I could tell him how safe he made me feel. About how lovemaking arising out of sleep was a revelation of two souls more open and giving, more purely present, free, and charged than in the bright light of day.

Only a moon's draught of space, a feather-beat of breath
is where our edges
Know this death.

I reach for my journal.

Dear Jim:

It's half-moon today. Eleven months since the day
you left. My throat aches when I wake. This, then, is what
the approach of the one-year anniversary is about.
Acceptance. As the nonreality of the past year moves
into certainty, a new kind of intensity builds. I stand
before a wall called Loss and I am about to climb over it
into new territory, and another season. The wall is not as
high as it was, yet it still has power. I'm not here on this
side with regrets or should haves, but just, in this one
moment of what had been: pure-empty-aching-
nonexistence-inexorable-unchanging-final-nevermore-
finished-over-done-the-end-deprivation-gone-loss.

This is the real end of that part of me that was you
here, your arms around me here, mine around you.
Here.

Silence. The room echoes.

I've been in a raw, learning place for a year. And now, I can feel my learning, my practices, my dreams, and my visions of a future solidifying and condensing into a new me. The crack between the worlds isn't as open or obvious anymore. My heart is freer now, without the heavy glove of sadness around it. Love can move.

The Christmas cactus from Jim's memorial is blooming—to excess, I think. It's too much, even in all its beauty. I feel slightly loosened in myself, partly the result of not sleeping well. I'm distracted and off center due to the push to earn money, the production of my latest writing, the heavy frost, and the moonlight hitting my eyes around 4 AM, plus the presence of the impending anniversary. Part of me is wound tight.

Work. Work. I know by now that things won't shift unless I also do the inner work.

I went to a Zen Buddhist meditation group yesterday evening. I'm inching toward finding a group with whom to practice. My old resistance to any kind of authority is getting in the way. The leader is young, twenty-nine, and I can't help myself: I want to challenge his youth. What can he teach me?

He shares a haiku in response to my question about combining Zen with my other spiritual questing.

He went angry into the garden,
And stopped to look at a red maple tree.

215

That works. My new life and a red maple tree strike a blow in my heart and I let it be.

NOVEMBER 12, 1994

I wake at 5:15 AM, the exact time Jim left a year ago.

Around 5:20, I feel my insides shift in a strange way, as if something inside me has lifted and taken off, the way Jim's spirit must have felt leaving his body.

Was the part of Jim in me leaving?

One year, and now we pass forward into new territory, he and I.

JANUARY 7, 1995

The waxing moon falls on my face and lights up a dream.

I have been voyaging to a place far across the sea and now I have come to the shores of my own country. My return will lead through a long, gray, stone tunnel, but now I'm looking back to see where I have been.

I see the rough waters I had to cross to come at last to where I now stand quietly, on the edge of a platform made of stone.

Far in the distance, through a mist, I can make out a very large, luminous, white building. It is rather Middle Eastern-looking. I had not realized that it looked like that.

I sense its great beauty and power.

Standing in the mouth of the tunnel and peering back through the mist, I can see that another crossing will not be easy.

I hear a voice: "It will be a long time before you go back there."

WHERE IS THE LAND OF THE DEAD?

Inside each of us
There is a world.

And inside that world
there is another
And inside of that
there is another
And another

And there are
So many, many
Worlds,
but
here's the thing:

Each world
Is Bigger
Than the last.
Now,
Finally,
we

come
to the
last
of all
possible
worlds.

And it is
the world
of the departed.

The Biggest World of All.

Inside material existence,
on a nonphysical plane,
countless beings
exist
in a very
tiny
space.

—inspired by the words of Sivaya Subramuniyaswami

SEEDS & STONES

NOVEMBER 12, 2022

THE REST FOR NOW

"Our souls aspire toward growth, that is,
toward remembering all that we have forgotten
due to our trip to this place, the earth."
—Malidoma Patrice Somé

Dear Jim,

I'm finishing our story on the twenty-ninth anniversary of your death. I am seventy-six now. I cannot begin to guess how old you are, because as I've learned, time has no meaning where you are.

These days you live inside me in a quiet, comfortable place. Only sometimes do you show up, around your birthday or on the date of your death, usually by sending me someone who is struggling, often with cancer. Then I share about us.

I remember well when I got an Apple computer, a few years before you died. You hated it with a passion. You were a Luddite, that's for sure. It was ugly, gray, with a tiny screen, and about the size of a breadbox. But I was all in—and it was hard not to be able to convince you that it was heating up happy visions in me of writing stories and essays like I did in my youth.

If you were still on the earth (instead of ever-becoming in your present reality), would you be amazed to read the posts on social media from the children who knew and loved us twenty-nine years ago? Or perhaps you already know that they are now around thirty-five and many have children of their own?

When I began writing about us, I did not really consider that those radiant kindergarten children would come to know the rest of our story. Back then, their innocence, imagination, and boundless creativity were our deep joy, constantly inspiring our own playful selves, which was the essence of what we loved about one another.

How is it now, for those same amazing, grown beings to read how the two teachers that they loved and respected back then, turned out to be complex human beings with both shadow and light in their lives?

I feel vulnerable, thinking of them reading about our pain and struggles. As I write these words for them and others to read, I hope they will be able to hear me now as a grandmother who treasures the memory of her time with them and hopes her words offer some inspiration and even guidance, despite the moments of raw pain and confusion I've shared.

I will now share the rest of the story about you, Jim, and our ducks, which I'm guessing you were waiting for me to mention.

* * *

Dear Now-grown children of Morningsong School, class of 1994,

The "phoenix" in a woodstove appeared again the year following Jim's death, also in May at almost the same time. Neither I, nor Marcus saw them. My daughter, Kyra, was the witness, who at that point was well established in her dream job as manager of the beautiful New Hampshire horse farm I've already mentioned.

One spring evening, she heard a knock on her door and opened to find an anxious-looking man and woman on her doorstep, whom she recognized as neighbors.

"We were going to light our woodstove," they said, looking helpless, "but when we opened the stove door, a duck jumped out and now it's running around our house! We don't know what to do. Will you come and catch it for us?"

So it was that my son, my daughter, and I were all touched by a serendipitous, symbolic message that new life will come again out of the ashes.

How does a river duck get into the body of a woodstove? I should clear this up. There are any number of wonderful ways to explain this phenomenon, one narrowly scientific, the rest mind-expanding and mysterious.

I will share two explanations.

First: As it happens, mergansers nest in natural tree cavities, big holes made by woodpeckers, rock crevices, hollow logs, and yes, sometimes in chimneys. And when the first and second ducks appeared inside two different woodstoves, a year apart, it was during their spring nesting time. I guess it's not a stretch to consider that on a cold and blustery day, a chimney opening looked like a very welcome place to begin a family.

This little bit of duck science is not to stick a pin in a balloon of wonderment and marvelous synchronicity. If a duck is going to represent a phoenix, I guess it would tend to be logical about timing with its own natural proclivities. Furthermore, such behavior had never occurred before in our life on the river, nor did it ever again.

Second: If Jim and Cinder the Cat could conspire to deliver me a nice fat mouse for my birthday, I'm fine with Jim and mergansers also making magic together. Especially because I hold in my heart the knowledge that in a shaman's world, ducks are powerful symbols of beings who can cross between the worlds of life and death, living in the two dimensions of water and air as they do.

Sacred messengers, feathers into the fire and reborn again and again, life to death to life once more.

* * *

About my dream to become a writer: I must report that my garden book did not find a publisher, although it came close twice. The lesson there is to never give up, but as you keep your dreams alive, trust that what's right for you might not be what you've planned.

I wrote arts reviews and opinion pieces for our local paper for about a year. On recommendation from writer friends, I began to do some magazine work. I also published some of my poetry and two essays were included in a collection about grief and loss.

But now I come to the good part: Remember my dream that was full of hundreds of dogs running down a big hill? And also, about the dowsing conference encounter with the spiritual dog trainer April Frost?

Susan Lee Cohen, my animal-loving literary agent, called me one day to ask how I was doing and then shared about a training problem she was having with one of her dogs. And I told her about April. We went together for an interview and April shared her unique method. Susan looked at me and said, "This is a big book and you are going to write it!"

And I did. Susan was able to negotiate a six-figure book contract for us, despite the fact that my resume as a professional writer could barely fill one sheet of paper. *Beyond Obedience: Training with Awareness for You and Your Dog* was published by Harmony Books, a division of Random House, the following year.

When I first got the news about the contract, I called my son Marcus, who was trying to make it as a writer in Hollywood. I shared the good news. And he replied, "That's nothing, Mom, I just sold a script for three times that amount!

Thus, the whole family had big dreams come true within three years after Jim stepped into his new reality.

Writing has become a way of life for me, always in the hope of finding good things to say about making the world a better place. In subsequent years, I worked on books (some published, some not) with a famous American witch, a bestselling American Buddhist, and a psychologist whose goal is to help people heal unresolved psycho-emotional parts of the self through understanding their spiritual roots and identity.

Then, the dog dream put out some more energy. Was it because the message was about unconditional love?

While I was working with April Frost on *Beyond Obedience,* I woke up one morning with this phrase in my mind:

A Dog is One Way
for God to Look
at You.

I did not know what it meant until ten years later, when I moved to the Pacific Northwest and I found myself experiencing the power in Dog Spirit when I focused on them through the lens of a camera. This inspiration became, for fifteen years, a successful greeting card company called

Lightmark Press, featuring my portraits of dogs in cars with humorous or heart-tugging captions.

Three years ago, I sold the business in order to work with my community on the climate crisis, for the sake of our children and the future of our magnificent Earth and her creatures.

This is my work today, which includes me contributing more writing wherever I can make a difference.

* * *

How to think about life after death: Was Jim a miracle worker? Or does all life contain miracles, described by Friar Giovanni Giocondo as a "living presence, woven of love, by wisdom, with power," and Jim and I were able to find a way to enter more fully into its mystery?

Western culture, said Rudolf Steiner, is in love with things. We believe in our possessions: that which we can see, own, hoard, and guard against theft or loss. The conventional view is that death is a loss, a failure, and healing from loss is generally defined as a psychological process, with the pain and stress of bereavement often managed with prescription drugs. This view and pharmacological solution bears heavily on how we grieve, it seems to me, perhaps leaving behind an abiding sense that some inner process has not been able to be completed?

Having spent time as a grief counselor for about five years before I moved to the West Coast, I was moved to discover how grateful my clients were when I suggested they might try creating a similar nighttime ritual like mine, while believing that it's possible to heal not by shutting down a connection with a departed loved one, but by practicing that love is eternal.

This is how I have come to think about the connection: There is a difference between being self-*conscious* versus self-*aware*.

Self-consciousness is about "I'm not good enough and I don't belong."

And self-awareness? "I trust and love because I'm not separate and alone."

Our culture is pathologically self-conscious, isn't it? And I would add, pathologically lonely. I now believe that humans have both a sense of self and a sense of extending beyond the self, into wholeness, and we have a word for each experience.

"But awareness is far more basic than words," writes parapsychologist Charles Tart. "If something survives death, it seems likely that it will be more closely connected with basic awareness than with ordinary consciousness."

My whole story then, is about how I moved from self-consciousness to self-awareness, which I experience not as a place you arrive in, but as an ever-evolving state.

I believe that the shock of losing Jim put me into a state of awareness that had great creative power and changed my life.

Today, I want to live in such a way that my sacred daily practice is to be present in life without limitations or judgments, putting my trust in the unpredictable. Which is me saying that no matter what the future brings, I deserve to be here—open, listening, with acceptance.

My stories: I wrote about the practice of allowing and intending. About clearing a night sky of clouds in order to witness a triangle of three brilliant planets. About holding Jim's head so lightly and lovingly in my hands until I could feel the invisible prickling of his pain subside and fall away. About freeing a calf's head stuck in a fence by not trying, but by letting some intuitive, subtle communication do the work.

Since I've been stuck on this phrase *allowing and intending* for years, I'm always delighted to find a version of it expressed in other ways as well. For example, I found this sentence by the theater critic John Lahr in an article about stage fright.

The paradox of acting is that, like surfing, it requires both relaxation and concentration. If there is concentration without relaxation or relaxion without concentration, the performance doesn't work.

My conclusion: Allowing and intending, or relaxing and concentrating, is another way to talk about entering, becoming, and participating in life, so that it flows through me, offers itself to me, without definitions or limits.

My practice is to intuit what feels right, act, and prepare to be surprised.

Which inspires me to end with one final story.

And I'm imagining Jim laughing—maybe because it's about life after death and a computer.

"Mary Bloom, Photographer to Dog Stars, Dies at 81"

In October 2021, the *New York Times* reported the death of my friend Mary Bloom. Her twenty-one years as a brilliant staff photographer at the annual Westminster Kennel Club Dog Show, her fierce passion for animals, and her generous spirit are legendary among those who knew her.

This is not a recounting of Mary's many accomplishments, however, but a true story for those animal lovers whose hearts also belong to Manhattan's Peaceable Kingdom, and who cannot bear to think about loss. I write to share what was known to only a few.

Mary was a firm believer in life after death.

When I visited Mary in May of last year, she asked for my help with an unusual task. She had saved the ashes of her cremated animal companions from over the years and because of the neuropathy in her hands, needed my help putting them into a vintage gallon-sized glass jar she had been saving for a special purpose.

We put on her favorite music, Pachelbel's Canon in D, and sat at the table, opening boxes, and then, plastic bags, containing the soft dust of Lucas, the African gray parrot, Kate, the dachshund, the yorkies Mighty Joe and Spanky, Fiona, the sheltie, and the cats Porch Cat and CeCe. As the ashes sifted together in the jar, there were some tears, but not many. Mostly gratitude.

I once said to Mary that I was afraid to get a dog, because I didn't know how I could deal with the inevitable ending. Her response was immediate and emphatic: "Dogs are made for love," she said. "To give love and to receive it. Why would you ever want to deprive one of its purpose?"

The jar was two thirds full when we finished. "There's just enough room still for Pie (her corgi) and me," said Mary.

I flew back home and in August, I called Mary for her birthday, but did not reach her. Some weeks later, we spoke and I learned of her cancer diagnosis. When not in pain, she reported she was busy sending out her handmade greeting cards, combining images, sometimes hers, sometimes recycled, always with a meaningful quote or two. Saying goodbye. "It's my time," she told me.

In October, she was gone.

In November, I was in my kitchen and my computer—which had been in sleep mode—suddenly woke and began singing an old song from the 1950's musical *Guys and Dolls:* "I love you, a bushel and a peck, a bushel and a peck and a hug around the neck." A pause. Then it would repeat. Over and over. I couldn't figure out how to make it stop. I finally had to shut the computer down, completely mystified.

I recognized the voice—it was mine, singing that song for someone on a voicemail. Befuddled, I didn't remember when I did it or for whom. I hadn't a clue how it ended up on my desktop computer since I had recorded the message via my iPhone. I left the mystery alone and went on with my day.

The following afternoon, I was once more in my kitchen and again my computer woke to sing "I love you, a bushel and a peck . . ." Once, twice, more to come. At which point, I suddenly knew. I went and stood in front of the screen and said aloud, my voice high and happy, "Is that YOU, Mary???" The song stopped.

Stunned moment. Then, "Well, you always did love computers, Mary," I said. And she really did—she was my go-to for all sorts of tech issues and had once worked in the industry. But how did she manage—wherever she was, to retrieve my voice on her iPhone and send it back to me on my computer? Because then I remembered that, in fact, when I called to wish her happy birthday last August, that song was the birthday greeting I had left for her.

Mary's last card to me included a Peanuts cartoon: "Someday we will all die," says Charlie Brown. "True, but on all the other days, we will not," says Snoopy. The card announces the death of her beloved Pie. "She's playing stick and ball and sniffing flowers in the clouds now!" wrote Mary. "Until I arrive!"

I think of Mary now as I near the end of my story, elder that I am. It's my time, said Mary, when death came and took her hand. "Why would we fear death?" asked Mary. ("Look, I'm still around," she has clearly demonstrated). She fully, generously, embraced life, and she acknowledged death as an equal partner.

If my journey to explore unseen worlds began with Jim, what journey begins when I meet him again?

***

What is the difference between seeds and stones? A stone is a history, a seed a promise. In this sense, we leave the stones behind as we journey towards healing.

But there is also a wider perspective to hold.

On the island of Iona, turquoise waves continually scatter the white sands with beautiful stones for pilgrims to find and treasure.

Birthed from the salt waters as they are, these symbolize eternity.

And they are also about renewal.

In a pocket, on an altar or a windowsill, or in a garden, they are not so much stones, as seeds of hope, found when one seeker bent over, took one up, and felt, despite her heavy heart, that her soul was awakening to beauty.

A small and vital moment telling of new life sprouting within.

ACKNOWLEDGMENTS

Since this book is a memoir that spans nearly thirty years, I close my eyes and see a multitude of faces of those who have come along with me on my journey, loving and supporting both Jim and me, and then me, after Jim. Deep love and gratitude to all!

My entire story of loss would have been very different were it not for the incredible strength, wisdom, and profound understanding of anthroposophical medicine brought to both of us by Dr. Anna Lups. She is truly an extraordinary healer in every respect.

Gratitude also to Dr. Quang Van Nguyen for his healing medicines and deep knowledge about how to understand and respect one's relationship with the dead. Also, to Margie Pivar, who introduced Jim and me to Quang and helped him publish his extraordinary life memoir, *Fourth Uncle in the Mountain.*

To my editor and book packager, Stephanie Gunning, for her wealth of know-how and bountiful capacity to support countless authors in realizing their dreams of publishing. It was my great good fortune to discover I'd saved her contact information for more than a decade—thus, 'twas fate to work together! Also, to Kristine Dahms of Twist Design, for sharing her award-winning talent as a graphic designer with me, producing a stunning book cover and cheerleading me on after kindly reading a draft of my manuscript.

To Susan Lee Cohen, since 1997 my literary agent and wonderful friend, who has kept me believing in myself over the years—a soul sister to be sure.

Gratitude to Stephanus Berard, Latin scholar, author, and generous host, who gave me a writing haven in his beautiful Whidbey Island home, complete with big view of the Cascade Range and the ferry crossing, plus great conversations, hikes, and movies on the weekend.

The children and their parents of Morningsong School, 1993, for their loving care and support, and especially kindergarteners Brigid, Mary B., and Lila, for their letters to me and Jim. The faculties of the Pine Hill Waldorf School and High Mowing School, who loved him and made sure he knew it.

To Ed Bartlett and Nik Keil, Jim's good friends and support during the hard time, also my great Vermont friends Terry Sylvester, Jillian Farwell, and Barbara Campman. To my Vashon readers, Carol Ellis, Margaret Roncone, Kristine Dahms, and Vashon supporters who read excerpts on Facebook and offered praise and advice. Gratitude for Vashon friendship and "book talk" to Susan McCabe, Sally Fox, Sheila Brown, Mary Van Gemert, and Lynn Greiner.

Special forever love for Madeline Thomson, who knows me better than anyone.

To the memory of Stella "Mammy" Chapman, her love for Jim and for me—never forgotten. To all of Jim's family, especially his sister, Barbara, and her husband, Eddie Lane.

To my beloved daughter, Kyra Gautesen, and son, Marcus Gautesen, and his family. To my inspiring sisters Kristin, whose beautiful smile and belly laugh are sorely missed, Andrea Scheidler, and Erica Swanson, and my brother, Jon Swanson, and their families.

Finally, to those you have read my story, and who also long to share yours: You can. And you should.

REFERENCES

THE FIRST QUESTION: BODY
WILL GRIEF KILL ME?

1: Moon in Dark Water
"An old verse about destiny and acceptance that I'd encountered in school." Adam Bittleson. *Meditative Prayers for Today, eighth edition* (Edinburgh, U.K.: Floris Books, 2017).

4: Wear Big Shoes
Epigraph. Michael Gellert. "Zen and Death: Jung's Final Experience," MichaelGellert.com (accessed January 29, 2023). A lecture first delivered in 1998.

5: Pendulum
Epigraph. Evelyn Francis Capel. *Understanding Death* (London, U.K.: Temple Lodge Press, 1987), p. 14.

9: A Room Full of Stars
Epigraph. John O'Donohue. *Anam Cara: Spiritual Wisdom from the Celtic World* (New York: Bantam, 1997), p. 276.

11: Where Is the Land of the Dead?
Epigraph. John O'Donohue. *Anam Cara: Spiritual Wisdom from the Celtic World* (New York: Bantam, 1997), p. 273.

12: Who to Wear

Epigraph. Pema Khandro Rinpoche. "The Four Points of Letting Go in the Bardo," Lionsroar.com (November 29, 2022).

15: Celestial Vitamins

"Red essence of the mother . . ." and the prescription for grieving. Sogyal Rinpoche. *The Tibetan Book of Living and Dying* (San Francisco, CA.: HarperSanFrancisco, 1993), pp. 314–15.

16: A Small Green Stone

Epigraph. Pema Chödrön. *When Things Fall Apart: Heart Advice for Difficult Times* (Boston, MA.: Shambhala Publications, 2000), p. 1.

19: Anticipation and Revelations

Epigraph. John O'Donohue. *Anam Cara: Spiritual Wisdom from the Celtic World* (New York: Bantam, 1997), p. 136.

Johann Sebastian Bach. "Ascension Oratorio," lyricist and translator unknown (debuted May 19, 1735).

20: Iona

Epigraph. Malidoma Patrice Somé. *Ritual: Power, Healing and Community* (New York: Penguin Books, 1997), p. 24.

21: The Difference Between

Epigraph. Rudolf Steiner (1861–1925). Translated from German by the author.

Roy Wilkinson. *Rudolf Steiner: An Introduction to His Spiritual World-view, Anthroposophy* (U.K.: Temple Lodge Publishing, 2001), p. 107.

Rudolf Steiner (lecture). "The Dead Are With Us," translation by D.S. Osmond, RSArchive.org. Lecture GA 182, delivered February 10, 1918, in Nuremberg, Germany.

THE SECOND QUESTION: SOUL
WHO AM I WITHOUT MY BELOVED?

22: Choices
Epigraph. Max Ehrmann. "Desiderata" (1927).

Ambroise Vollard. *Cezanne,* translated by Violet M. MacDonald. (Boston, MA.: Little, Brown and Company, 1936).

23: From Noun to Verb
Epigraph. Nathaniel Hawthorne. *Passages from the English Note-Books of Nathaniel Hawthorne* (1870).

25: Closet of Dreams
Epigraph. Carl Jung. *Dreams.* Dreams: (From Volumes 4, 8, 12, and 16 of the Collected Works of C. G. Jung) (Jung Extracts, 34) Bollingen Series XX.

26: Breakthrough
Epigraph. Willa Cather. *Death Comes for the Archbishop* (New York: Vintage Classics, 1990), p. 50).

28: Salt Mines
Epigraph. C.S. Lewis. *A Grief Observed* (New York: HarperOne, 2015), p. 56. Originally published under the pseudonym N.W. Clerk in 1961.

29: Not Really Here?

Epigraph. Henry Wadsworth Longfellow. "Chapter 6: Glimpses into Cloud Land," *Hyperion, Book 2* (1882).

30: Not Your Fairy Godmother

Epigraph. Carlos Castaneda. *Tales of Power* (New York: Washington Square Press, 1974), p. 133.

32: Jim Paints Me

Epigraph. Mary Ellen Mark. *On the Portrait and the Moment: The Photography Workshop Series* New York: Aperture, 2015).

33: Finding the Fire

Epigraph. Rabindranath Tagore. *The English Writings of Rabindranath Tagore: Poems, Vol. 2* (2007)

Roy Wilkinson. *Rudolf Steiner: An Introduction to His Spiritual World-view, Anthroposophy* (U.K.: Temple Lodge Publishing, 2001), p. 107.

34: The Other Side of the Hedge

Epigraph. David Spangler, spiritual director of the Lorian Association. Notes from a lecture I attended some years ago.

35: A Question of Naming

Epigraph. Lois McMaster Bujold. *Cordelia's Honor* (Wake Forest, N.C.: Baen, 1996).

C.S. Lewis. *A Grief Observed* (New York: HarperOne, 2015), p. 63. Originally published under the pseudonym N.W. Clerk in 1961.

36: Interwoven, All the Same
Epigraph. Joan Erikson. *Wisdom and the Senses: The Way of Creativity* (New York: W.W. Norton & Company, 1991).

THE THIRD QUESTION: SPIRIT
WHAT IS MY SOURCE OF STRENGTH?

37: A Living Presence
Epigraph. Friar Giovanni Giocondo. Letter to Countess Allagia Aldobrandeschi sent on Christmas Eve, 1513.

39: Source of Strength
Epigraph. Pierre-Simon, marquis de Laplace (1749–1827) was a French mathematician, astronomer, and physicist who studied the solar system. These are his last words, as reported in Joseph Fourier. *Elonge Historique de M. le Marqus de Laplace* (1829).

"Man is his own star . . ." John Fletcher, "Upon an Honest Man's Fortune" (1647). According to Misha Teramura, the poem was published "as a paratext to the play *The Honest Man's Fortune* (1613)": "Archival Reflections: The Fortunes of Fletcher's 'Against Astrologers,'" *Modern Philology*, vol. 118, no. 1 (August 2020).

Viktor E. Frankl. *Man's Search for Meaning*, translated by Ilse Lasch (Boston, MA.: Beacon Press, 2006), p. 38. Originally published in German in 1946.

Anton "Bert" Hellinger (1925–2019) was a German psychiatrist. These remarks came from a lecture I attended for a certification in Family Constellations therapy in 1999.

Rainer Maria Rilke. *The Notebooks of Malte Laurids Brigge*, translated by Stephen Mitchell (New York: Vintage International, 1990), p. 19.

42: Divination
Epigraph. Paulo Coelho. *The Alchemist, 25th Anniversary Edition*, translated by Alan R. Clarke (San Francisco, CA.: HarperOne, 2014), p. 39.

Chapter 43: If You Can See It
Epigraph. Paracelsus. *Neun Bücher Archidoxis* (circa 1529).

48: Where Is the Land of the Dead?
Sivaya Subramuniyaswami (1927–2001). Born Robert Hansen, and known to his followers as Gurudev, he was an American Hindu religious leader. Notes I took after a lecture.

SEEDS & STONES: NOVEMBER 12, 2022

49: The Rest for Now
Epigraph. Malidoma Patrice Somé. *Ritual: Power, Healing and Community* (New York: Penguin Books, 1997), p. 22.

Friar Giovanni Giocondo. Letter to Countess Allagia Aldobrandeschi sent on Christmas Eve, 1513.

Charles Tart, "Who Survives? Implications of Modern Consciousness Research." In Gary Doore, editor. *What Survives? Contemporary Explorations of Life after Death* (New York: J.P. Tarcher, 1990), p. 144.

John Lahr, "Petrified: The Horrors of Stagefright," *New Yorker* (August 28, 2006), p. 39.

Richard Sandomir, "Mary Bloom, Photographer to the Dog Stars, Dies at 81," *New York Times* (October 13, 2021), p. B11.

ABOUT THE AUTHOR

Rondi Lightmark (RondiLightmark.com) lives on Vashon Island in the Pacific Northwest, and can be found most days in a colorful, very small cottage with a desk, cupboard bed, and tea kettle or her nearby garden. She holds a master's degree in psychology from Saybrook University and has been an educator, school administrator, grief counselor, professional photographer, and, since 1996, professional writer. Her first book, cowritten with dog trainer April Frost, which is entitled *Beyond Obedience: Training with Awareness for You and Your Dog*, introduced the concept of using visualization to empower training cues. It was the first of its kind to teach this approach.

Rondi has worked as a writer for both Omega Institute and Esalen Institute, America's two leading holistic and educational retreat centers. In 2005, she launched Lightmark Press, a popular greeting card company featuring her graphic arts images of dogs in cars, combined with her humorous or poignant captions. In 2019, she sold the company and created the Whole Vashon Project (WholeVashonProject.org), using education and the arts to unite the Vashon Island community around working on the climate crisis. She is dedicating the rest of her writing life to this effort.

Made in the USA
Las Vegas, NV
18 February 2023